November 2006

For Ed + Mary Anne —

THANK YOU FOR ALL YOUR SUPPORT
AND HELP. I AM GLAD YOU ARE
ABLE TO SHARE THIS SPECIAL DEDICATION
WITH US.

BEST WISHES
YOUR FRIEND
Marcel S...

LETTERS ON THE WALL

FOR ED SANDT — U. S. ARMY —
THANK YOU FOR YOUR COMMITMENT AND DEDICATION
TO SERVING OUR COUNTRY. YOUR BRAVERY, HONOR + COURAGE
ARE A TESTAMENT TO THE GREATNESS OF OUR
NATION AND OUR ARMED FORCES.

THANK YOU FOR ALL YOU HAVE DONE.

"THEY ARE NOT JUST NAMES ON A WALL"

✳ Smithsonian Books   Collins
An Imprint of HarperCollinsPublishers

MICHAEL SOFARELLI

LETTERS ON THE WALL

Offerings and Remembrances from the Vietnam Veterans Memorial

PICTURE CREDITS:

All photos, unless otherwise indicated, printed with permission
and courtesy of the Vietnam Veterans Memorial Fund.

Janet Evans-Scanlon: p. vi. Panoramic Images/Getty Images:
pp. x-xi, 200. VVMF/Tom Estrin: pp. 191-193. VVMF/Daniel Arant:
p. 194. Terry Adams–NPS: p. 196. VVMF/Mariah Payne: p. 199.
Izzy Schwartz/Getty Images: p. 200.

U.S. Navy emblem used with permission. Neither the Department
of the Navy nor any other component of the Department of
Defense has approved, endorsed or authorized this publication.

"Father's Day at the Vietnam Veterans Memorial," by LTC Anthony
V. Fasolo, used by permission of the author.

HarperCollins books may be purchased for educational, business,
or sales promotional use. For information please write: Special
Markets Department, HarperCollins Publishers, 10 East 53rd
Street, New York, NY 10022.

Published 2006 in the United States of America by Smithsonian
Books in association with HarperCollins Publishers.

Designed by Janet M. Evans-Scanlon

The Library of Congress Cataloging-in-Publication
Data has been applied for.
ISBN-10: 0-06-114877-6
ISBN-13: 978-0-06-114877-4

For my father,
who gave his blood, sweat
and tears for his country.
Semper Fi.

And for my mother,
who stood beside him
every step of the way.

And to all our men and women who
have protected and served this great
country, past, present and future. . . .
Thank you! And welcome home.

MAN • ROBERT L HARLEY • JOHN L SMITH • MICHAEL
N L STEVENSON • KENNETH R BUELL • VERNE G DONNELLY • THOMAS A GOETS
MAS O ZORN Jr • ROGER W CARROLL Jr • DWIGHT W COOK • TIMOTHY J SWEEN
PETER CHAN • VINCENT C ANDERSON • RICHARD B LINEBERRY • ROBERT A BRET
MAN • SCOTT L BIRKET • HERMAN C ACKER • JACK S BERGMAN Jr • WILLIAM CLAR
RONALD P DALEY • RAYMOND R DAVIS • TERRY W DEAL • WILLIAM H HARRISON
BERT M KIKKERT • ROBERT T MOORE • EDWARD R McELENEY Jr • STANLEY G PILO
NSON • WESLEY H ROSE • RICKY LEE RUCKER • JEFFREY L SCHELLER • DAVID L SCO
RICHARD C TESSMAN • JOSEPH GRISAFI • ROBERT D ANDERSON • BRUCE E BOL
K • PETER M CLEARY • LEONARDO C LEONOR • FRED G MICK • JOHN R PEACOC
JAMES L CRAIG Jr • JAMES D DUGGER Jr • ALLEN U GRAHAM • JAMES A HOCKRID
HAEL S BIXEL • CLAYTON M BLANKENSHIP • DANIEL P CHERRY • ROBERT A YANKO
N Jr • KEVEN Z GOODNO • CARLOS A PEDROSA • MELVIN E WOLFE • JAMES W H
D OBERDING Jr • JAMES E SULLIVAN • JAMES D BROWN • RAYMOND L GOODCH
S W FINNEGAN • RICHARD B FREEMAN • LOUIS O CALDERON • MILTON C HUN
ES A McSWINEY Jr • KENNETH J SPENCER • JAMES M STEVER • CHARLES L STEWA
RONALD L VANLANDINGHAM • DAVID E WISCHEMANN • HOWARD W JOHNSO
LIAM L MILLER III • STEVEN L TAYLOR • JOSEPH F DE NARDO • CLARENCE O TOLB
N L CARROLL • ROBERT D MORRISSEY • FREDERICK W WRIGHT III • RONNIE N TO
NALD C BREUER • CHARLES J CAFFARELLI • WILLIAM S HARGROVE • ROBERT A KO
ONALD D STAFFORD • CALVIN B TIBBETT • WALTER H TRISKO • CHARLES M EARN
Y M JONES • RICHARD E BRUNDRETTE Jr • ANTHONY C SHINE • MICHAEL S McN
LIE JOE WILLIAMS • BILLIE JOE WILLIAMS • WALTER L FERGUSON • JAMES R McELV
L • ROBERT J THOMAS • RONALD J WARD • RICHARD W COOPER Jr • DONALD A
S X EGAN • CHARLIE S POOLE • LARRY D SCHUMACHER • ARTHUR V McLAUGHLI
PAUL • RANDOLPH A PERRY Jr • WARREN R SPENCER • JOHN F STUART • JOEL R BIR
RANDALL J CRADDOCK • CHARLES E DARR • DELMA E DICKENS • ROBERT T ELLIC
ER • JAMES R FULLER • FRANK A GOULD • ROBERT S GRAUSTEIN • THOMAS T HAR
ARD H JOHNSON • BOBBY A KIRBY • JOHN Q WINNINGHAM • HARRY R LAGERW
GEORGE B LOCKHART • ROBERT R LYNN • PAUL O MEDER • GEORGE D MacDONA
T • ROLLIE K REAID • BARTON S WADE • FRANCIS A WALSH Jr • DONOVAN K WALT
ALD W ALLEY • THOMAS W BENNETT • JOSEPH B COPACK Jr • WILLIAM R BAIL
DY H • HAROLD L MISCHLER • HENRY J REPETA • GEORGE F SASSER • D
EN RAYBURN • DWIGHT G RICKMAN • ROBERT J MORRIS • D
RALPH CHIPMAN • RONALD W FORRESTER •
SILVER JAMES M TURNER • BENNIE •

1959

IN HONOR OF THE MEN AND WOMEN

OF THE ARMED FORCES OF THE UNITED STATES

WHO SERVED IN THE VIETNAM WAR.

THE NAMES OF THOSE WHO GAVE THEIR LIVES

AND OF THOSE WHO REMAIN MISSING ARE INSCRIBED

IN THE ORDER THEY WERE TAKEN FROM US.

OUR NATION HONORS THE COURAGE,

SACRIFICE AND DEVOTION TO DUTY

AND COUNTRY OF ITS VIETNAM VETERANS.

THIS MEMORIAL WAS BUILT WITH PRIVATE

CONTRIBUTIONS FROM THE AMERICAN PEOPLE.

NOVEMBER 11, 1982

1975

CONTENTS

PREFACE

For me, an artwork begins when I finish it.

The work comes to life as people interact with it. Still, I could never have imagined how very physical that interaction would be at the memorial and how moving it is to see the extremely personal objects and heartfelt thoughts left at the Wall.

Letters on the Wall beautifully captures the emotion and tenderness of these objects. It offers a very powerful and intimate response to the memorial.

I was truly touched by this book.

—Maya Lin,
Architect, Vietnam Veterans Memorial

FOREWORD

There are books that simply need to be written. *Letters on the Wall* is one of them. This book is not just a moving tribute to the Vietnam Veterans Memorial—it does an admirable job at capturing much of the very essence of the profound emotions and living history that the Wall stands for as a unique icon—one with near religious qualities—in contemporary American society.

At the Wall, many deep, private encounters take place between the living and those whose names are engraved thereon. I have seen many of these communions with those who will be *forever young* as the result of the Vietnam War. Indeed I have had my own encounter.

In 1992, I visited the memorial with National Public Radio correspondent Alex Chadwick. He asked me to take him to see the names of some of my friends. It was painful to do this. But a decade after the memorial had been built, it was time.

It was January 1970. There was an explosion and a truck loaded with ammunition caught fire. Fearless American soldiers, most of whom were draftees, ran to the burning truck to remove the wounded—most of whom were dying. Others put out the fire.

As I finally faced the names of my friends, I relived the incident which brought me nightmares for many years. Those who were there on that day cannot hold back their tears when discussing the soldiers whom we were unable to save.

Maya Lin brilliantly placed the names of the fallen in chronological order on the memorial. In this way, those whom died together rest together on the Wall for as long as our nation exists.

It is painfully obvious that *Letters on the Wall* is not just for those who served in Vietnam. This book will help all Americans to better understand the bonds of loyalty of those who serve in our nation's military forces. These bonds of loyalty, courage, and duty are not unique to Vietnam, and this book helps explain in a profound manner why those in our armed forces show such bravery and risk their lives.

I was honored recently to be with a group of soldiers who took heavy casualties on a mountain peak in Afghanistan. A Navy Seal was surrounded by Taliban. The rescue troops landed and fought through the evening—outgunned and outnumbered by hundreds of experienced fighters. American losses were heavy.

They found the Navy Seal the next day. He had been killed in action. Yet no one regretted trying to save him; they all wanted to try—at the risk of their lives. And so it was on other battlefields—at Gettysburg, at Iwo Jima, and at Bunker Hill. American servicemen and servicewomen fight for our nation, but in battle they fight for each other with a bond of friendship that is not just close, but as *Letters on the Wall* illustrates, extends beyond the grave.

Our nation is usually divided over various politically charged issues. In good faith, we use our democracy to argue our beliefs and make our values known to others in what Oliver Wendell Holmes called *the marketplace of ideas.* Yet we do stand together to honor our fallen.

In a stirring speech, Holmes, a decorated veteran of the Civil War, wrote:

BUT GRIEF IS NOT THE END OF ALL. . . . I SEE BEYOND THE FOREST THE MOVING BANNERS OF A HIDDEN COLUMN. OUR DEAD BROTHERS STILL LIVE FOR US, AND BID US THINK OF LIFE, NOT DEATH—OF LIFE TO WHICH IN THEIR YOUTH THEY LENT THE PASSION AND JOY OF THE SPRING. AS I LISTEN, THE GREAT CHORUS OF LIFE AND JOY BEGINS AGAIN, AND AMID THE AWFUL ORCHESTRA OF SEEN AND UNSEEN POWERS AND DESTINIES OF GOOD AND EVIL OUR TRUMPETS SOUND ONCE MORE A NOTE OF DARING, HOPE, AND WILL.

There is an inspiring and poignant quality to the work of Michael Sofarelli. You will enjoy this book. You will be moved and you will better understand all who did their duty and all who do their duty today for our nation.

—Jan Craig Scruggs, Esq.,
Founder and President,
VIETNAM VETERANS MEMORIAL FUND

As a young boy I visited the Wall with my family. My brother and I were too young to understand why we were there. And more than likely, we were too excited by the large crowd of people gathered at the Wall to give much thought to its significance.

Now I know why we were there. Now I understand why we went. We were there to find my father's friends.

Growing up, I often wondered what it was about that Wall, that big black wall of granite that affected people so powerfully. A Wall made total strangers embrace each other. A Wall that could break down the toughest soldier and reduce him to tears. I remember seeing grown men cry as they touched the Wall, as they ran their hand over a name. Who was that person? Why did it make that man cry when he touched his name?

That day, I remember seeing my father touch a name. I remember watching my father cry, my mother, too. Whose name was that? How did they know him? I later learned that it was the name of the soldier my father had on his MIA/POW bracelet. They had found him on the Wall. They had touched his name.

My father, Michael Sofarelli Sr., was a United States Marine who served in Vietnam. Like many before and after him, he served his country and served it well. One February night in Vietnam in 1967, his platoon was attacked. During the firefight, a grenade was thrown at them. It bounced off another Marine and landed inches from my father, where it exploded. My father's right leg was very badly damaged and it had to be amputated. He took shrapnel in one eye that now limits his eyesight, both of his eardrums were blown out, and he had numerous gunpowder burns that covered his body. He was nearly killed.

It was the Wall that made me realize my father had almost been killed. This was something I would struggle with for some time. The fact that he had come so close to dying ate away at me as did the question of why my father got to come home when so many others did not. So many fathers gone, so many potential sons and daughters lost. But now, in a strange way, it is the Wall that has helped me to heal—as it has helped so many others.

In 1996, I went back to the Wall. It was not a planned visit, just part of a spur-of-the-moment stroll through D.C. one evening. I went not knowing that my life was about to change dramatically. As I walked through the memorial, a strange feeling of tranquility came over me. The sun was fading, and it was getting dark. There were only two other people at the Wall. They were at the opposite end from where I was standing. From a distance, I watched what appeared to be a father and his young son. They were pointing at a name. The man touched it. And then, the little boy put something on the ground. I watched as they walked away. As quickly as I had noticed them, they were gone.

I walked over to see what they had left.

At the base of the Wall where they had been standing was a small piece of paper. I knelt down to look at it. In a child's handwriting, the red crayon read simply, "Happy Birthday Grandpa." At that very moment, I realized how precious life is, and how very fast it can be taken away from us. If the grenade that wounded my father had landed inches closer to him, I would not be standing in front of this monument; instead my father's name would be on it.

I was twenty-two then. The same age as many of the soldiers whose names appear on the Wall, the same age as my father when he enlisted as a Marine. There I stood, alone in front of the Wall that had once raised so many unanswered questions. And now, all the questions had returned. "Who was that person?" "Why is his name there?" "Why did that name make that man cry when he touched it?"

I walked closer to the Wall, closer than ever before. And for the very first time, I touched the Wall. I touched a name. A name I did not know. For the very first time, I cried at the Wall.

I finally understood.

INTRODUCTION

In 1982, when the Vietnam Veterans Memorial was under construction, a United States naval officer walked up to the Wall's foundation, where concrete was being poured. He paused above the open pit and then tossed something into the wet concrete. After a moment of reflection, he stood at attention, saluted, and then walked away. A workman yelled out to him to ask what he had thrown into the concrete. The officer said he was offering his dead brother's Purple Heart to the Wall, and walked away.

This act began the phenomenon of leaving remembrances at the Wall.

The dramatic and somber Vietnam Veterans Memorial sits between the Washington Monument and the Lincoln Memorial on the Mall in Washington, D.C. The Memorial, more commonly known as the Wall, was dedicated in November 1982. Since that time, the public has left letters and objects of remembrance every single day. At first, park rangers did not know what to do with these items, but in 1984 they began to save and catalog them. Every night, park rangers and volunteers collect and inventory each item, noting the date and location where the item was left; then they place the items in plastic bags. Approximately fifteen to twenty-five artifacts are left on a typical day. On holidays like Memorial Day, Veterans Day, and Father's Day, as many as one thousand items are left.

These gifts of remembrance are cataloged and preserved by the National Park Service in the Vietnam Veterans Memorial Collection. The collection, which now numbers well over 75,000 items, is stored in a climate-controlled environment in the newly built Museum Resource Center in Maryland. The collection houses thousands of pieces of traditional military memorabilia such as flags, medals, uniforms, boots, MIA bracelets, and dog tags. In addition to these more traditional items, the public has left teddy bears, baseballs, money, pictures, firearms, keys, cigars, and even a Harley-Davidson motorcycle.

Most numerous, however, are the written mementos, including poems, greeting cards, notes, and letters. At the Wall, the term "letter" may take on a new and unusual meaning. There are traditional letters written on paper or stationery and sealed in envelopes. But much of the written correspondence takes on more inventive forms.

Letters have been written on everything and anything imaginable. Any item that has personal meaning and represents the loss, the pain, and often the guilt of war has been used: a hat with a message of forgiveness from one veteran to another, a photograph and message of good-bye for lost lovers who were never able to say farewell, a flag that honors those who are still lost, a beer can and bottle of whiskey from a soldier paying up old debts and having one last drink with a buddy, a child's diaper, a rock, a knife, a leather vest, sneakers, and even an egg have served as material for letters and tokens of remembrance. Many of the stories and objects are offerings from soldiers who survived to those who did not. All remember a loved one or friend in a unique and meaningful way.

Many believe the Wall is a place where veterans can find closure, and find the courage to confront and speak of their experiences. Many describe it as "the wall that heals." The Wall has become a sacred place, allowing veterans to reflect, remember lost friends, and, in many cases, heal old wounds.

Originally the memorial was intended to honor those who were killed or missing as a result of the Vietnam War. However, since its dedication in 1982, the memorial has also had a powerful impact on many others among the four million people who visit annually. Many have no direct connection to the war but frequently they are stunned by the sheer magnitude and sense of loss associated with the Vietnam War and the Wall. More often than not, a person will walk down into the memorial and walk up a changed person.

THE VIETNAM VETERANS MEMORIAL

The Vietnam Veterans Memorial was established by the Vietnam Veterans Memorial Fund (VVMF), a nonprofit, charitable organization founded by a group of Vietnam veterans and led by Jan Scruggs, who served in Vietnam from 1969 to 1970 as an infantry corporal. Jan Scruggs and the VVMF raised nearly $9 million entirely through private contributions from corporations, unions, foundations, veterans and civic organizations, and close to three million individual Americans. No federal funds were needed for the Vietnam Veterans Memorial. The walls and landscaping were completed by November 1, 1982. The Vietnam Veterans Memorial Fund then officially transferred control of the memorial to the National Park Service, a division of the U.S. Department of the Interior. President Ronald Reagan accepted the completed Vietnam Veterans Memorial on November 10, 1984. The next day the wall, the statue, and the flag were recognized as one national memorial.

The Vietnam Veterans Memorial, designed by Maya Ying Lin, then an undergraduate architecture student at Yale University, consists of four elements. The Wall, the first part of the memorial to be erected, was dedicated on Veterans Day, November 13, 1982. The Wall actually consists of two distinct walls: one pointing east toward the Washington Monument and the other pointing west toward the Lincoln Memorial. Each wall is 247 feet long, and each is composed of 70 separate granite panels that reach a high point of more than 10 feet at their geographic center. On the panels are inscribed the 58,249 names of soldiers killed or missing as a result of the Vietnam War. There are eight women. Approximately 1,200 of these names are listed as MIA (missing in action). Each panel is 40 inches in width, and each of the largest panels has 137 lines of names inscribed on it. Each line contains five names, with each name depicted with either a cross or a diamond next to it. The diamond represents KIA (killed in action), while the cross represents MIA. The cross, which has no religious meaning, was chosen so that if a missing soldier's remains were found, it could be carved easily into a diamond. If a missing soldier is found alive, a circle is to be carved around the cross. To this day, no circles have been inscribed on the Vietnam Memorial Wall.

As with the Vietnam War, the memorial dedicated to it was not without controversy. Many felt that the Wall did not honor Vietnam veterans appropriately. Many veterans felt that the memorial did not reflect the heroism and patriotism depicted by other war memorials in and around Washington, D.C. Some veterans felt that a memorial belowground that focused on death was inappropriate and insulting. Although the memorial was funded with private money, it had a vast political fallout. A letter signed by twenty-seven Republican congressmen stated, "We feel this design makes a political statement of shame and dishonor rather than an expression of our national pride at the courage, patriotism, and ability of all who served." President Reagan did not attend the original dedication ceremony. Once again, America was divided over the Vietnam War.

In 1982, a compromise was reached and a statue was commissioned. The *Three Servicemen* statue was to be the second element of the memorial. The Vietnam Veterans Memorial Fund selected sculptor Frederic Hart. During the summer of 1984, Mr. Hart's sculpture was cast in bronze by Joel Meisner. The three figures depicted wear Vietnam-era uniforms that could represent any branch of service. The lead soldier was actually modeled after a twenty-one-year-old Marine stationed in the Washington, D.C., area at the time the sculpture was being designed. The soldier, wearing a military bucket-style hat and carrying a machine gun, was modeled after a Cuban American. The African American soldier, who holds a rifle at his side, is a composite of several men that the sculptor used as models. The statues show the men emerging out of the woods, looking confused, tired, and vulnerable. They stand closely together, yet each one seems strangely alone. They look directly toward the apex of the wall, located approximately 140 feet away. These figures were unveiled on November 8, 1984.

Some interpretations of the work claim that the servicemen have the "thousand-yard stare" and are looking past the memorial. Others have said that the troops are on patrol as they protect their lost comrades on the Wall. Some believe they are ghostly figures emerging from the woods looking for their own names on the memorial.

Nearby a sixty-foot flagpole flies an American flag twenty-four hours a day, seven days a week in honor of the men and women listed on the Wall. At the base of the flagpole are the seals for each of the five branches of military service: Air Force Army, Coast Guard, Marine Corps, and Navy. On the base is the following inscription:

THIS FLAG REPRESENTS THE SERVICE RENDERED TO OUR COUNTRY BY THE VETERANS OF THE VIETNAM WAR.

THE FLAG AFFIRMS THE PRINCIPLES OF FREEDOM FOR WHICH THEY FOUGHT AND THEIR PRIDE IN HAVING SERVED UNDER DIFFICULT CIRCUMSTANCES.

In conjunction with several special ceremonies at the memorial on Memorial Day, Veterans Day, and POW/MIA Recognition Day, a POW/MIA flag is flown on the same staff underneath the United States flag.

The third element of the Vietnam Veterans Memorial is the Vietnam Women's Memorial. This was conceived by former Army nurse Diane Carlson Evans and designed by sculptor Glenna Goodacre. It honors all women who served in Vietnam. The statue depicts three uniformed women nurses surrounding a wounded soldier. One nurse comforts the wounded warrior, while another kneels nearby. The third looks skyward. Some interpret this third nurse as looking for help and awaiting a helicopter; others suggest she is looking toward a higher power or perhaps questioning the great cost of war. The Women's Memorial was dedicated on Veterans Day in 1993.

The newest addition to the memorial site is the In Memory plaque, known formally as the Vietnam Veterans Memorial Commemorative Plaque. The two-foot-tall by three-foot-wide granite stone plaque sits within the Three Servicemen Plaza and is inscribed with:

IN MEMORY OF THE MEN AND WOMEN WHO SERVED IN THE VIETNAM WAR AND LATER DIED AS A RESULT OF THEIR SERVICE. WE HONOR AND REMEMBER THEIR SACRIFICES.

Because of policies set forth by the Department of Defense, these names are not eligible for inclusion on the Wall. Creation of the In Memory plaque was authorized by Congress in April 2000, the bill was signed into legislation by President Bill Clinton, and the plaque dedicated on November 10, 2004.

THE LETTERS

My Marine:

There is no name for me to touch and run my fingers over to ease the pain. Oh, it is here, somewhere, among the thousands between 1969 and 1971; and you are but one of the hundreds who, for all our skill and all our trying, we could not mend. The only difference is that they are a part of an endless parade of wounded broken bodies and you, you alone, are the one I remember.
You are the one for whom I grieve.

I was off that day, if you can be off on twenty acres surrounded by barbed wire in the middle of nowhere. They came and took me away from a good book to see "the other head wound." Ike, the other neuro Doc, was getting the first one ready for surgery and you and I would be up next. So off I went to receive another bloody mess into my hands as I had done every day, many times a day, for over a year.

There you were, eighteen years old, blond crew cut, blue eyes, a tan that said "I am no cherry." You were covered in the accumulated grime of days in the bush. you were in no pain, you were lucid. You could move all extremities, and someone had to point out the mosquito bite size entry wound of a piece of shrapnel on the back of your head.

I got x-rays and took them in for the neurosurgeon to look at. There was no hope. The shrapnel had entered your head and run around your skull like a ball in a roulette wheel. Damage to the brain would cause swelling and death, operating was useless. It had taken us months to get the 'cherry' neurosurgeon to stop operating on hopeless cases, tying up an operating room for hours, while those who could be helped waited, and sometimes died in the waiting. I had fought hard and long for this approach and you were the classic case.

You would be dead in three hours, in a coma within two. You were to be hooked up to a heart monitor, made comfortable, and I was to stay with you until the monitor straight lined. You were mine.

I was twenty-five years old, and old man in Nam. I was into my second tour, back to back, a long time in Nam. I was trained in surgery, where people are asleep, have no individual identity are referred to as the part of the body being operated on, "the arm in #3," "the leg in #5" and "the head #6." But you, you were awake, alive, an individual, and even to me at twenty-five, only a boy.

It was decided not to tell you that you were dying. Was that the right choice? I think that is what haunts me the most. We made it, I stuck to it. Wille Nelson sings that "there is nothing I can do about it now" and in a way that song has set me free; that and the fact that I believe your mother, knowing that your last hours were free of worry and sadness, would have approved.

It was only a scratch. You would be back with your buddies tomorrow, no sweat.

It was hotter than hell so I got some marines to put you in pre-op, one of the few places with air conditioning. We got your utilities off and you took a sponge bath, the first in eight days you said. We talked and laughed and smoked.

What we spoke of, your name, where you were from, of these things I remember nothing. For me you were, and are, Viet Nam. All the wasted lives, for no purpose. Not one of us would leave undamaged. All would be forever changed by the experience of "NAM," and you, you would be dead.

In the third hour you went to sleep, you never woke up. Thirty minutes later your heart stopped. You died in peace, in ignorance that your life was at an end. How I wish I could tell your mother. How I wish I could touch your name and say goodbye.

My mother used to say that when we die God sends someone to greet us when we get to heaven. I hope God sends you, and I hope you will tell me your name. Until then, you are my Marine and I will always remember you.

DOC

Michael

1st Med Bn
1st Mar Div
I Corps
Da Nang, RVN

OR 28 CHRISTMAS MORNINGS
I THOUGHT OF YOU AND OUR
LAST CIGAR TOGETHER

OW FOR YOUR BIRTHDAY IT'S TIME Fo
YOU TO CATCH UP TO ME

FRANCIS EUGENE SANDERS 32
6-12-48 — 12-25-67

HAPPY BIRTHDAY AND UNTIL NEXT
CHRISTMAS MORNINGS CIGAR AND I PR
THERE WILL BE MANY MORE

GOD KEEP YOU – YOU ARE NOT FORGOTT

SGT. J. KORNSEY
D 3/503 173RD ABN.
67-68

FRANCIS G PATTON

To our uncle,

Love
from
The Patton Kids

"AN OPEN LETTER TO BY BROTHERS"........

THIS MARKS THE 3RD TIME I HAVE COME TO THE WALL.
I HAVE SEEN THE NAMES OF THOSE I KNOW AND YES, I HAVE CRIED.
MY PROBLEM IS I DON'T KNOW THE NAMES OF THOSE I TRIED TO HELP
ONLY TO HAVE THEM DIE IN MY ARMS. IN MY SLEEP, I HEAR THEIR
CRIES AND SEE THEIR FACES...... IN VIETNAM, AT AGE 18,
I WAS PUT IN CHARGE OF A RIVER BOAT. NOW EVERYTIME I GET ON A
BOAT I ONLY SEE THE RED BLOOD RUNNING OVER THE DECK AND INTO
THE WATER!!!

        I WRITE TO SAY I'M SORRY!!! TO ALL YOU, MOTHERS, FATHERS,
BROTHERS, SISTERS, WIVES AND LOVERS OF THESE MEN!!!
"I'M SORRY"!! "I COULD DO NO MORE"!!   I CAN COUNT THE NUMBERS,
112 MISSIONS TO BE EXACT. MY BOAT WAS ALWAYS FIRST, I MADE SURE
OF THAT. YOU KNOW, NEVER SEND ANYONE SOMEWHERE YOU WOULDN'T GO
YOURSELF. I WISH I KNEW YOUR NAMES SO I COULD TOUCH YOUR NAMES
IN THE BLACK STONE. BUT I DON'T, AND I'M SORRY! "SO SORRY"!!!

        ATTACHED TO THIS LETTER ARE MY SERVICE RIBBIONS..........
I DON'T NEED THEM TO SHOW I WAS THERE!!!
I HAVE YOUR FACES TO REMIND ME IN MY SLEEP.......
I WILL LEAVE NOW TO RETURN TO MY SAFE PLACE. MY GIRLFRIEND, WHO
HAS STUCK BY ME FOR THE LAST FEW YEARS, SHE WAS THERE FOR ME!!!!

        REST WELL.... MY BROTHERS....
        MAY THE WIND BE TO YOUR BACKS AND THE SUN IN YOUR FACE!!!
ON THE DAY WE MEET AGAIN, PLEASE DO ONE THING!!!

        "TELL ME YOUR NAME"!!!!

                                LOVE, YOUR BROTHER,

ROGER "PIPER" PEIFFER
RIVER PATROL FORCE
TF-116 PBR-571
VIETNAM "68-69"

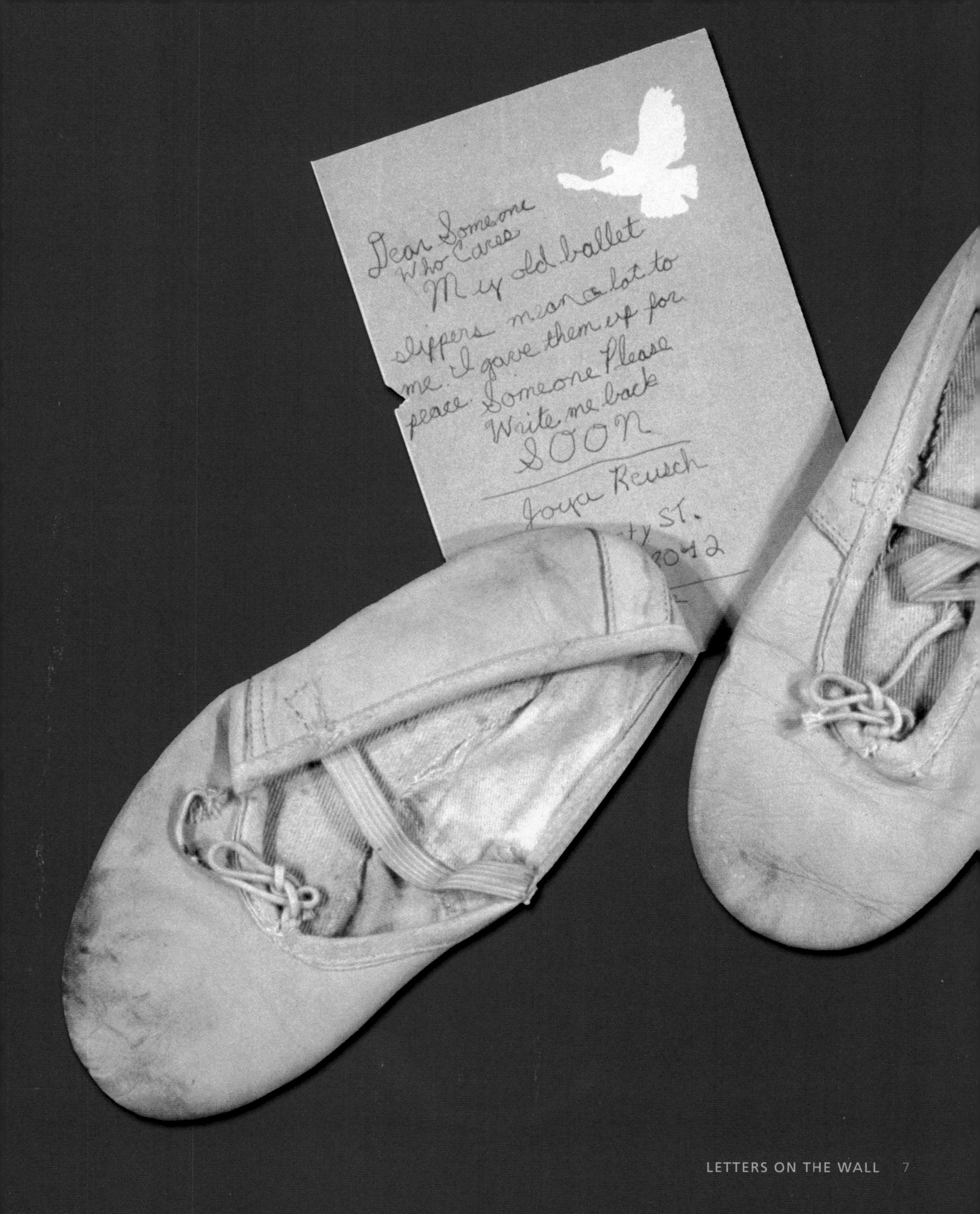

Dear Someone
Who Cares
My old ballet
slippers mean a lot to
me. I gave them up for
peace. Someone Please
Write me back
SOON
Joya Reuch
_____ty St.
_____2012
_____

DEAR MICHAEL—
HERE'S SOME BEER TO
GO WITH THE FOOD AND
THE SMOKES (SORRY,
NO BA MUOI BA IS
AVAILABLE IN RALEIGH).
BERNIE BIRENBAUM'S
(3E52) GOT THE SMOKES
AND EDDIE BLUMER'S
(29E38) GOT <u>REAL</u> FOOD.
LOVE, Jeff 8/5/94

LCPL EDWARD E. BLUMER, USMC
1st Marine Division
Died Of Wounds
Danang, South Vietnam
7 November 1967

DEAR EDDIE
HERE'S SOME <u>REAL</u> FOOD
(NO "HAM AND MOTHER'S").
BERNIE BIRENBAUM'S
(3E52) GOT THE SMOKES
AND MICHAEL BERDY'S
(32E61) GOT THE BEER.
LOVE, Jeff 8/5/94
CPL. JEFF KANNER
1ST MARINE DIVISION
DEC. 66 - DEC. 67

TRIBUTE TO A VIETNAM VET

This is a tribute to all of you who died so vallantly, in a war that was not your own; yet you died anyway. I leave this patch as a gift from all of those who were there with you but are yet alive today. To thank you for your sacrifice. I am sad that you had to die but thankful that I (1st Cav Combat Medic) still live after two tours in the hell that was Viet Nam. It is my prayer that todays Army is not called to task. Should they ever be, it is my fervent hope that they will fight as gallantly as those of us who did what the weaker would never dare to do. To walk where those so critical would never be brave enough to walk. To see things that those of lesser character could never bear to see. To feel the putridness of fear in the bowels of your soul, and yet walk on to a mission you did not choose.

May your souls find peace in death, among the highest angles of heaven, that did not exist in your last tortured moments upon the earth.

Oct 86

The Words still won't come to express the LOAD I still carry, We were so young when we went and so old when we returned. It is too painful at times to Remember, but it is a pain that I carry with Pride & HONOR today

To My fallen Brothers of the Night, The Words still won't come, but then Maybe NONE Need to be Spoken.

USMC.
Chu Lai
1966-1967
LCpl Romus D. Tiskus

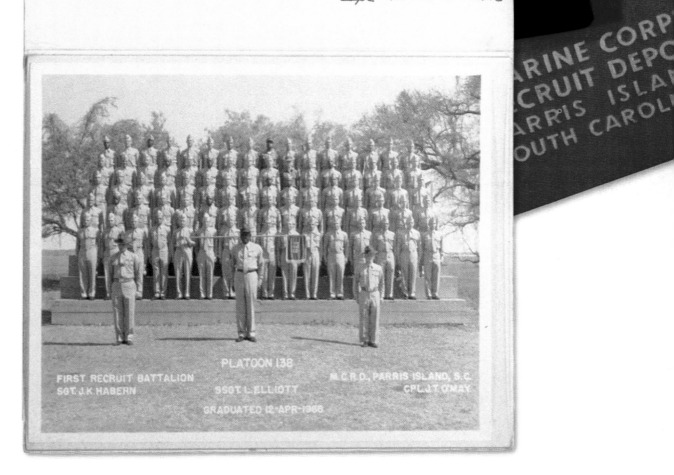

PLATOON 138
FIRST RECRUIT BATTALION   M.C.R.D. PARRIS ISLAND, S.C.
SGT. J.K. HABERN   SSGT. L. ELLIOTT   CPL. J.T. O'MAY
GRADUATED 12-APR-1966

May 27, 1986 1:30am

To: LCDR Barton S. Wade, USN

From: John H. Truesdale (USN 1964-1968)
(formally of the Veteran's Vigil for POWs/MIAs)

Dear Sir,

I never knew you, or you, me. You came from my mothers home state of Indiana, you from Jasper, my mothers family from Muncie. I am returning the bracelet I wore with your name on it. Last March I recieved the news that you had returned home after being shot down over North Vietnam Dec. 12, 1972. Welcome home, Sir.

For you, Sir, the war is over. For many of us it will never be, over. Many questions of what if, if we had done this, or should we done it differently, go through our minds, would it have made any difference? The one question I have now is; how long were you a POW before you died? Nobody will ever know. Will they?

I'm sorry I did not attend the public events yesterday. One, because I can't take large crowds, and two, because I don't think my emotions could hold up. But after watching Nightline (ABC) on TV lastnight about the wall and such. I felt such shame for not being here, that I cried, alone, for an hour before starting this letter. I'm sorry, Sir, I let you down, I let my buddies from the riverboats, who didn't come home alive, down, and, I let the three Truesdale family members on the Wall, down. And, I let myself down.

Five Truesdales from this grand old Northern Irish clan (first generation settled near Pittsburg in 1771 and fought beside Gen. Washington), that I know of, served during Vietnam. Two came home, my Daddy and me. My father was a Col. in the Marines, and was fifty years old when he went in 1969. I was 21, an"old man" by most standards then in 1968. Three didn't make it home, alive.

> SSG Stanley E. Truesdale USAF (Panel 1 east, line 25)
> SSGT Larry Lee Truesdale USA (Panel 2 east, line 90)
> SP5 Charles Kenneth Truesdale USA (Panel 13 west, line 124)

Three cousins I never knew, but I still cry for them.

But, why should I cry? You, Sir, and they will never know the cold and heartless world we came home to. Will never recieve the thrill of being refused jobs because of your service background. Or being rejected by the VFW and/or the American Legion because "we don't want any drug crazed 'Nam Vets in our Post". Or even the thrill of having your emotions jerk you up and down like a yo-yo until you finally go the the psycho ward and "pop smoke", because you could no longer handle it. You missed out on all that good stuff, I didn't.

You will never experience the failures many of us have had. Myself? Yes, I lost my business in '82, my house in '83, my marriage and my sanity (or what was left of it) in '84. BUT, I still survive and WILL survive. Why? I don't know. I sometimes joke that I'm so far out that neither one of the two factions that deal in the afterlife want me, and I doomed to be immortal. Because I have done so many things, then and recently, that should have resulted in my death. But, death has escaped me. So, I'm here for the duration gang, sorry.

In seven months, I will be forty. Wow. Most times I don't feel that old. Sometimes, I must admit, I feel a hundred and forty, mentally (I think most of us aged a hundred years overseas), and physically (sp?)(these old bones creak, pop, and jam). And the world is looking better every day. And if life begans at forty, I can't wait, because the first thirtynine have been pure S--T!

And get this, Sir. I'm going to get married again. And this one WILL work, she is as beautiful inside as she is outside. She does not harp on my failures, as my last wife, but spurs me into doing better next time and grabbing the brass ring on the next time around.

As I have put on the heading of this letter, Sir, that I am formally of the Veteran's Vigil. I resigned last month for many private reasons, but I'm not giving up on the still missing from the war. I will be back from time to time, not being aligned with any group around the Wall, but will help out where ever I can. I miss my watch from 0700 to 1500, Sundays. I miss talking with the people that came by, the families of the KIAs, the families of the MIAs/POWs, and my brother veterans.

I will be back, Sir. Because a part of me, my life, is engraved on these black stone walls. They were my friends, my buddies. We ate, slept, drank, laughed, cried and fought together. Now they are gone and I'll never see them in this world ever again, ever. A part of me is dead, it died over there, like so many of us. In a country that I never heard of until the summer of 1965 when then President Johnson put the whole fleet on alert, a year and a half after I enlisted. But it's still dead, and I haven't felt like a whole person for eighteen years, almost half my life. They are gone, a part of me died with them. But, I'm still here, and I miss them.

But, I swear, as long as I'm still alive. I will never let the world forget what the politicians, the media and the Hollywood types that gave their blood to the North did to us. They should be tried for nearly killing off an entire generation of young American men and women. Too many of us bear the mental scares of their mis-directed power and fame. These 58,132 will, along with myself, not let them forget it, Sir. I promise.

And when I finally do leave this world, Sir. My final wish will be that my boonie hat shall be placed at the apex of the Wall, showing that I have finally gotten away from that part of history and have joined my shipmates in whatever lies beyond.

But, for now, Sir. I'm going for the brass ring, ain't nobody gonna stop me either. I'm gonna make it, for you guys who didn't get the chance. I'm going to make this second marriage work, come hell and/or high water. I'm tired of being kicked in the ass by the world, I'M kicking back, you wait and see, Sir.

Anyways, Sir, here is your bracelet back. I'm now wearing one for CDR Gene A. Smith, USN, shot down over North Vietnam twenty years ago a month from now (6-27-66). Maybe I can help bring him home to.

Again, Sir, welcome home. You did, give everything you had, your life.

JERRY MYSELF, RICK

DAD,
THIS IS YOUR ONLY GRANDCHILD AND
YOUR NAMESAKE - I KNOW HE
WILL CARRY IT PROUD & THAT YOU
WOULD BE PROUD - IT'S SO HARD TO
REMEMBER YOU AS DAD - THAT I
CAN'T IMAGINE YOU AS GRANDAD - BUT
I KNOW YOU WERE A WONDERFUL-
LOVING DAD AND WOULD BE ONE OF
THE GREATEST GRANDPA'S EVER.
LOVE + MISS YOU ALWAYS -
                Karen & Robbie
9 MO. (MAY 92)
            1 YR (AUG '92)

3 MO (OCT 91)

To my
favorite cowboy daddy
"NOBOL" aka daddy
I love and miss
you always!
George

POW MARCH 18, 1968
(Not Yet Returned)

"HAPPY BIRTHDAY SON"

DAD & STEPMOTHER JEAN

BORN NOV. 10 1949

S/Sgt JAMES MICHAEL RAY

V.V.M. WALL   45 EAST   LINE 28

9 November, 1992

Dear Louis,

I write this letter to you as a way of releasing your spirit. We have been together as flesh and spirit since September, 1966. I think that I now have the strenght to go on with my life so I can now release your spirit. I do this with both joy and regret.

My friend, we went through our medical training together at Ft. Sam Houston, Texas and then went to Vietnam to serve our country. I had just turned 18 and was terribly afraid. You were older and wiser. You gave me hope for survival, picking me up when I was down. You never critisized when I was not the bravest of the brave. I owe you much.

I tried to reach you on the day you needed me but found only your empty shell. Your spirit left your body and has been near me, with me, these many years.

There were times when the bad spirits tried to saddle me with guilt but your spirit was with me and again saw me through. I was never alone. You stayed with me until I could stand on my own. I can now release your spirit to God and heaven. I know you will receive a heroes welcome in heaven. You are a hero.

I leave my vest for you and our other fallen brothers as a sign of my gratitude. The patches and ribbons are a sign of our times and the Vietnam experience that we all endured. If there is any envy or respect that goes with these patches and ribbons of our past, it belongs here with you and the other spirits that honor these walls.

I will never forget you Doc Castillo. Rest in peace my friend.

Love,

"Doc" Nordan

These Brave Marines Were Killed in Action in Helicopter Valley 20 years ago on Operation Hastings. They Were Killed While Carring Wounded To Safety. They Were Brave Men Doing a Brave Deed Under Fire on a Day When Courage and Heroism Were The Norm. Now Their Names Have Faces on This Memorial For All To See and Remember. Memories of Them Will Be in My Heart + Mind For The Rest of My Life. They Were In My Squad.

9 E 51
    52

Cpl Don Miller
3rd Squad 2nd Plt.
"I" Co 3/4

Dennis L. Harmon — Left

Douglas R. French — Right

Dear Neil: May 26, 1986

We never had the chance to meet, and I have never known the joy of your company.
Still, I feel an inner need to talk and share a few thoughts with you on this occasion.

As I stand here before your name and all the others, surrounded by countless other
individuals remembering shared happiness and expressing profound sorrow, I am moved to
tell you how I feel. First, I feel honored and proud that you sought to defend us and
our beliefs, even when some of us weren't really sure of what those beliefs were.
You knew. You knew what was right and saw your duty clearly. For that perception and
selfless devotion to us, we can never thank you enough. We can build memorials and
erect statues from dawn to setting sun, but we could never equal what you have given
us - your most precious possession, your life.

I also feel angry - angry because you were denied what so many of us take for granted,
the opportunity to live out our lives in the manner of our choosing. You never raked
leaves in the back yard of your own home, saw one of our own walk on the moon, or
heard a small, sweet voice call you "Daddy". What about the rest of us? We can no
longer feel uplifted by your smile, warmed by your touch, or awestruck by the
wonderful completeness of things as we watch you sleep in front of the TV. Those eyes
of yours - we miss those beautiful eyes that we could look into and feel your essence
without having to speak, those eyes that gently transformed our gaze into the best
that we were, and returning it to us tenfold, having been filtered with love through
your caring mind. Yes Neil, it hurts. It hurts very much.

Despite the hurt and pain, I am also gratified. I'm glad you had the brief time with
us that you did, and had the chance to feel the happiness, and yes, the occasional
sadness of growing up in a small New England town. I think what comforts me the most
is the fact that you had something a great many of us never get the chance to
experience - you found someone who loved you very much, a life-partner you could
love in return and share an all-too-brief life together with. There is no force
stronger than love, and you had the chance to know the intense joy of loving and
being loved by another precious human being.

Mary Lou is doing well, Neil. She has two beautiful children, a promising career,
and is now married to a man who is perhaps my dearest friend. You'd like Brian,
I think - if nothing else you both share a deep and abiding love for a truly
remarkable woman. I know that you would want her to be happy, content and loved.
I can tell you that she is all of these things, although she will always love and
miss you in her own special way.

Finally, as inadequate as it sounds, I want to thank you - thank you for being the
man you were, for sharing yourself with us, and for doing what you did in our name.
You were more of a man than I could ever hope to be, and your dying has forever
changed our living. Countless are the times when we wanted to hold you just one
more time and tell you how very much we loved you; to hear you laugh again;
to share your tears; but of course that cannot be. What can be are the moments
you occupy in our hearts and in our minds - they are very special indeed, my friend.

                          Thank you, dear one -
                          you are deeply loved and greatly missed.

                                              - Lester W. Paquin

For NEIL ROBERT BURNHAM, SP4 Army, born March 8, 1948; deceased December 17, 1968,
from Petersham, Massachusetts (Panel 36 on the West Wall, Line 33) - on the occasion
of Memorial Day, Monday, May 26, 1986.

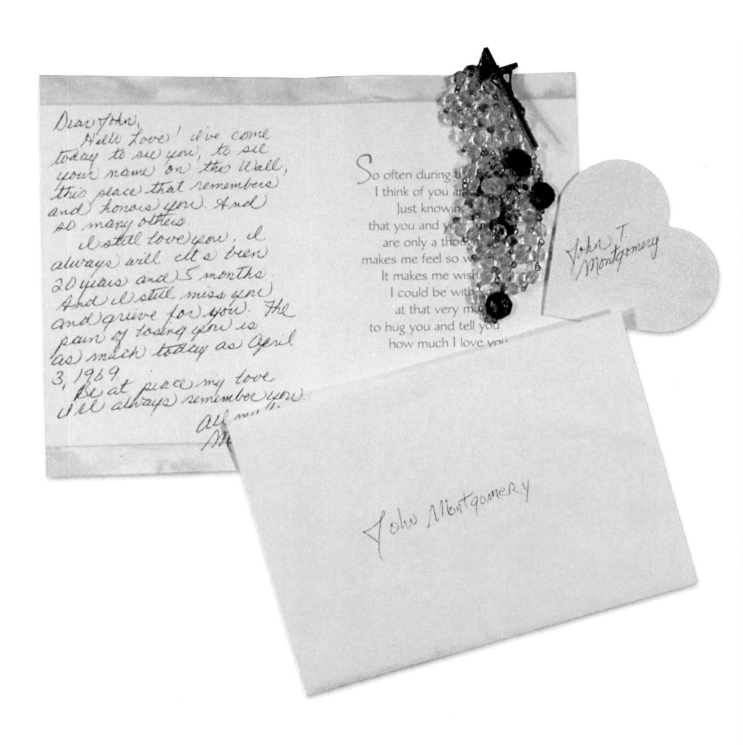

Dear John,

Hello Love! I've come today to see you, to see your name on the Wall, this place that remembers and honors you. And so many others.

I still love you. I always will. It's been 20 years and 5 months. And I still miss you and grieve for you. The pain of losing you is as much today as April 3, 1969.

Be at peace my love. I'll always remember you.

All my l.
Me

So often during th
I think of you a
Just knowing
that you and y
are only a thou
makes me feel so w
It makes me wish
I could be with
at that very mo
to hug you and tell you
how much I love you

John T.
Montgomery

John Montgomery

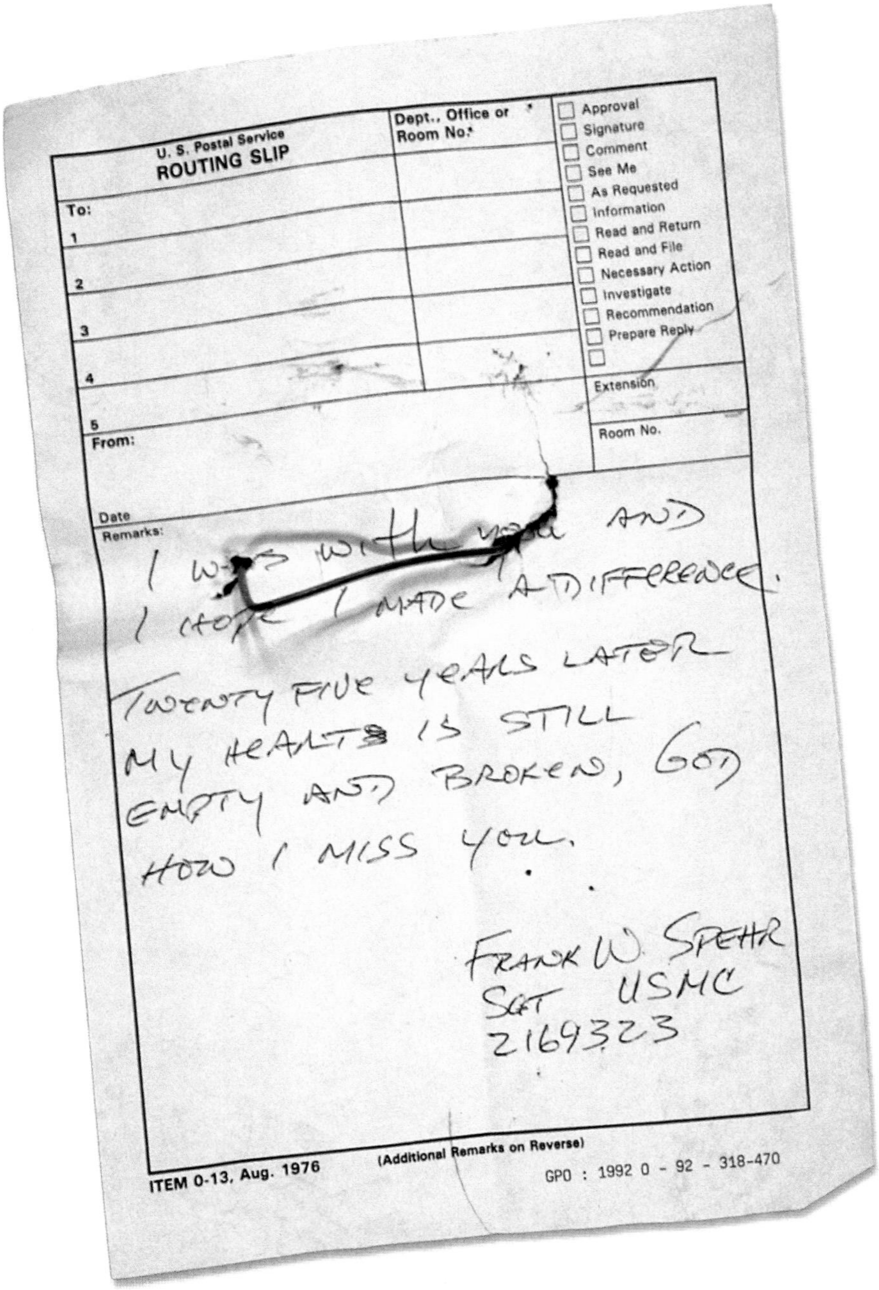
U. S. Postal Service
ROUTING SLIP

To:	Dept., Office or Room No.*
1	
2	
3	
4	
5	

- [ ] Approval
- [ ] Signature
- [ ] Comment
- [ ] See Me
- [ ] As Requested
- [ ] Information
- [ ] Read and Return
- [ ] Read and File
- [ ] Necessary Action
- [ ] Investigate
- [ ] Recommendation
- [ ] Prepare Reply
- [ ]

From:

Extension

Room No.

Date

Remarks:

I WAS WITH YOU AND
I HOPE I MADE A DIFFERENCE.

TWENTY FIVE YEARS LATER
MY HEART IS STILL
EMPTY AND BROKEN, GOD
HOW I MISS YOU. . . .

FRANK W. SPEHR
SGT USMC
2169323

(Additional Remarks on Reverse)

ITEM 0-13, Aug. 1976

GPO : 1992 0 - 92 - 318-470

Dear Ralph,
I'd like you to know that
you are well remembered.
I don't you well but I am
very close with you.
your Buddies didn't let you
down they still love you.

I remember
you with honor
& bravery

JBE

FEELINGS

THE VIETNAM WAR IS INSIDE ME
I FIGHT BUT I CAN'T GET AWAY.
THE PAIN OF MY FRIENDS WHO DIED BESIDE ME
ARE STILL WITH ME EVERY DAY

I TRY TO HIDE MY HATE AND MY SORROW
BUT THE PAIN SEEMS TO NEVER GO AWAY
THE MEMORIES AND FACES ARE WITH ME
THEIR SCARS ARE WITH ME TO STAY

I WENT TO NAM IN THE 60's
TO DO WHAT WE THOUGHT WAS BEST
BUT AS COMBAT INFANTRY SOLDIERS
WE WERE GIVEN AN IMPOSSIBLE QUEST

ALL OF MY FRIENDS WERE MY BROTHERS
WE WALKED THROUGH THE JUNGLE AS ONE
WE WATCHED AND LOOKED OUT FOR EACH OTHER
IN A WAR THAT COULD NEVER BE WON

GOING TO NAM GAVE LIFE MORE MEANING
BUT THE MEANING IS STILL NOT RIGHT
BECAUSE WHEN I SLEEP
MY FEELINGS ARE SO DEEP
THAT IN MY DREAM I STILL FIGHT

Sept. 3, 1992

Dear Marlin,
    Remember the last time I saw
you + you showed me those magic
card tricks? You told me that
when you got back from Nam, you
would show me how to do them.
Well, you never came back, + no one
else has taught me how to do those
card tricks.
    Well, these cards are for you.
And from where you are, keep looking
down on me.

                    Your cousin,
                    Kathy

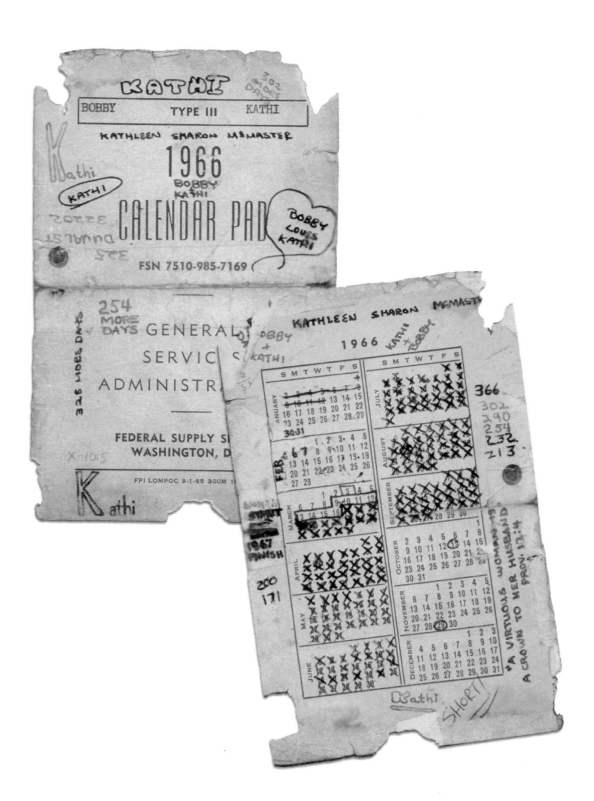

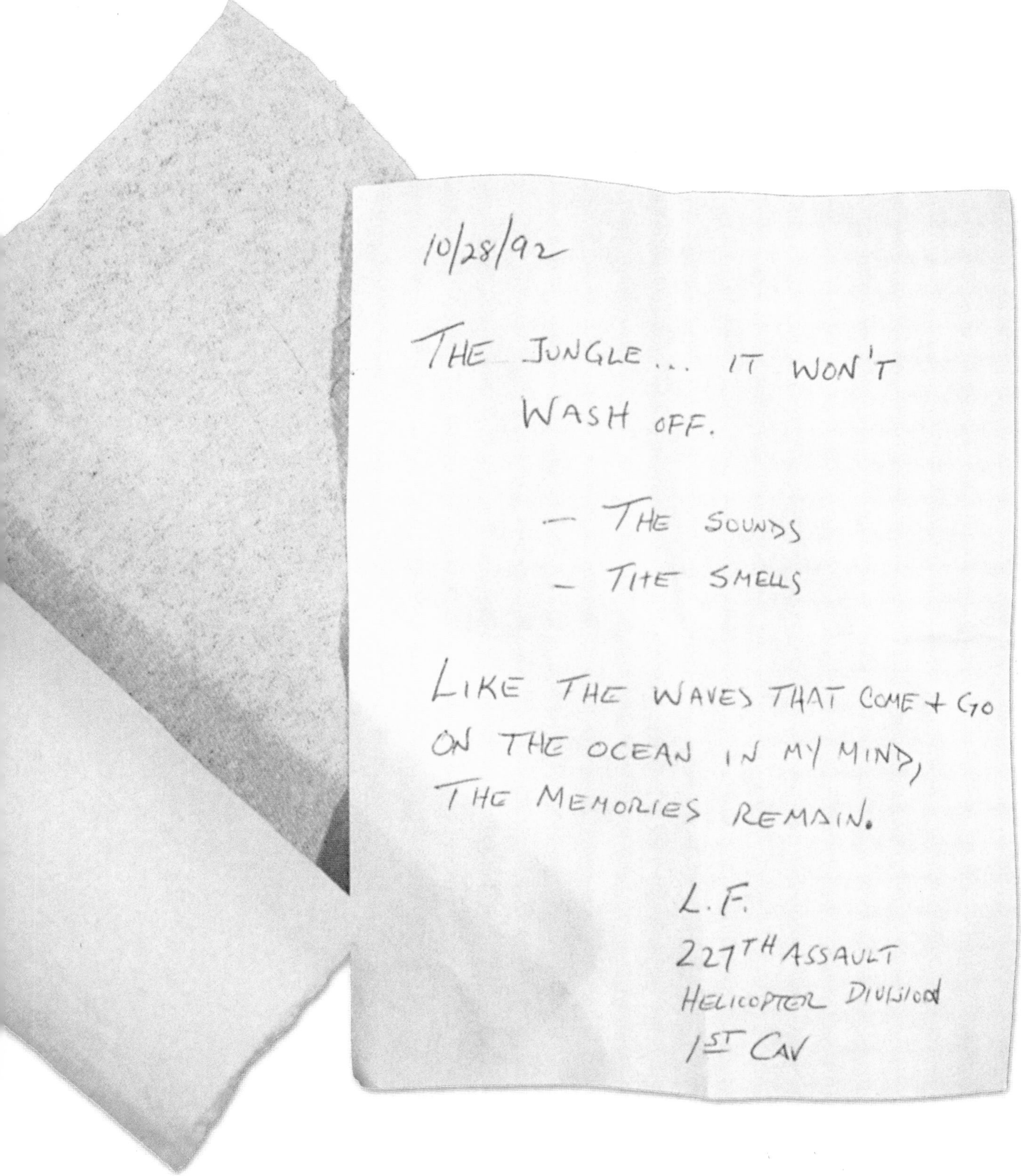

10/28/92

THE JUNGLE... IT WON'T
WASH OFF.

    — THE SOUNDS
    — THE SMELLS

LIKE THE WAVES THAT COME + GO
ON THE OCEAN IN MY MIND,
THE MEMORIES REMAIN.

    L.F.
    227TH ASSAULT
    HELICOPTER DIVISION
    1ST CAV

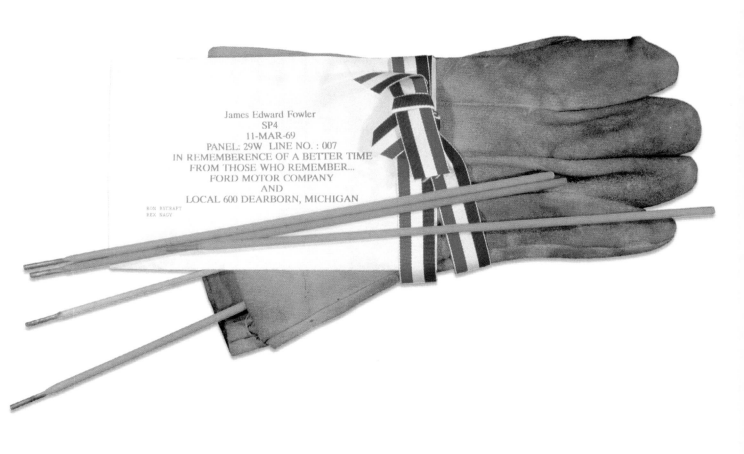

James Edward Fowler
SP4
11-MAR-69
PANEL: 29W LINE NO. : 007
IN REMEMBERENCE OF A BETTER TIME
FROM THOSE WHO REMEMBER...
FORD MOTOR COMPANY
AND
LOCAL 600 DEARBORN, MICHIGAN

RON RYCRAFT
REX NAGY

The UNITED STATES MARINE CORPS - over
210 years of romping, stomping, hell,
death, and destruction ... the finest
"fighting machine" the world has ever
seen!

I was born in a bomb crater 'n whelped
on "RBC" - my mother was an M60 and my
father was the Devil. I'm a roguish,
roving soldier-of-the-sea. I'm cocky,
self-centered, overbearing, and I don't
know the meaning of fear for I am fear
incarnate! I'm an air-cooled, C-rat' &
beer propelled, green amphibious monster
with a cast-iron belly and a rubber bung
hole!

I crawled up from the bottom of the
briny sea - and my sole function in life
is to wreak untold death 'n destruction
on pus-ridden anti-Americans 'round the
globe! Every heartbeat that I live is an
additional threat to YOUR life....
Whenever it may arise, and when my time
draws nigh, I'll die gloriously for God,
'Corps, 'n Country.

We stole the Eagle from the Air Force,
the Anchor from the Navy, and the Rope
from the Army ... and on the Seventh
Day, while God took his pack off, we
overran his perimeter 'n stole the Globe
... 'n we've been running the whole show
ever since! We live like soldiers, talk
like sailors - 'n slap the hell outta'
both of 'em! Soldier by day, lover by
night, drunkard by choice - 'n a MARINE,
by God!

AUG-12-'92 WED 08:33 ID:MACHINE SHOP   TEL NO:217 283 8361   #446 P02

ERNEST L. ROWE
1966 HOMECOMING DANCE

You're never
gone from our thoughts
or
HEARTS.

The flag reads:

25th ANNIVERSARY
USMC-Viet-Vet
Class of '67
L/CPL FRANK Martin Pietras
KIA - July 4th 1967 - The DMZ's
Meat Grinder - Operation Buffalo

This WWI Cap is a gift of Love from a mother of a Viet Nam Veteran who was KIA in 1968 the father was KIA in 1942. Will they ever learn when will we ever learn. Love Willie 67-68 Looper

With Love, understanding and hope will we be able to say - No more war!!
  Paul P. Stallings
  65-68

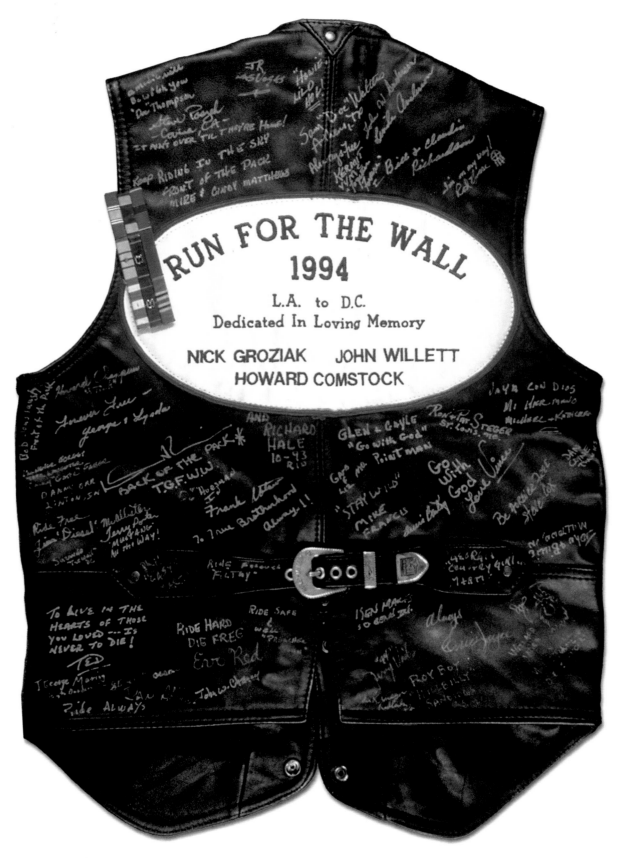

```
                    MIKE BADSING
                       USMC
                   KIA 6 SEPT 65
                    2E LINE 76

MIKE IT'S BEEN 27 YEARS SINCE YOU WERE KILLED IN VIETNAM.

IT HAS BEEN LONGER THAN THAT SINE WE PLAYED FOOTBALL TOGETHER
AT ST. EDWARDS, GRAMMAR SCHOOL. I STILL SEE YOUR MOTHER AT
MASS ON SUNDAY'S AND WE OFTEN TALK ABOUT YOU.

MIKE YOUR NEPHEW, YOUR BROTHER ED'S SON, BART REALLY LOOKS A
LOT LIKE YOU.

WE ALL MISS AND LOVE YOU MIKE, GOD BLESS.

A CLASSMATE, AND A FELLOW VIETNAM VET, ARMY 1965  1966.
```

CHIEF NURSING SERVICE
24th EVAC ...
A.P.O. SAN ... 8

CHIEF NURSING SE...
24th EVAC, HOSPITAL
A.P.O. SAN FRANCISCO 96291 1970

10 april 1986
I salute all my Vietnam
veterans friends !!
Ramona C. DeLairey USA,
Col, army nurse cops Retired
El Paso, Texas

VIETNAM
EXCHANGE PHOTO SERVICE VIET...

William James Rohan
HM3-USN FMF-USMC
KIA 16 September 1966
Panel 10E Line 103
We went through it all
together, Bill, then you
died in my arms in paddy
mud. I live my life for you
and Stormy. I'll never
forget you. Semper Fi, Bill.
Doc Luigi F Co. 2nd BN
7th Marine Regt 1stMARDIV

Gale H. "Stormy" Felver
HM2-USN FMF-USMC
KIA 29 July 1966
Panel 9E Line 86
You were always there for
all of us, Stormy. You
gave your life for me that day.
I live these days for you
and Bill. I'll never forget
you. Semper Fi, Stormy.
Doc Luigi F Co. 2nd BN
7th Marine Regt 1stMARDIV

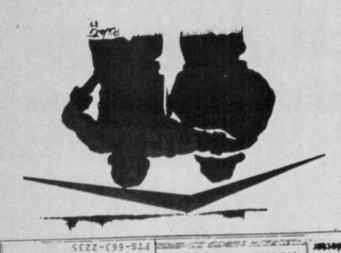
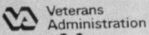

THE JUDGE

Continuation of Pontiac's mid-size supercar. Based on GM's corporate "split wheelbase" intermediate body/chassis design that debuted this year, with two-door models mounted on the shorter 112-inch span. GTO maintained its familial resemblance to the big Pontiacs, particularly in front with an oversize bumper/grille covered in soft Endura body-color plastic. Beginning in 1969, Pontiac offered "The Judge" package, with 366-bhp Ram-Air V8 and Hurst shifter, plus identifying front-fender decals and low wing spoiler on the decklid. GM finally rescinded its edict against intermediates with fewer than 10 pounds per horsepower for the 1970 season, and Pontiac duly made its largest 455 V8 a GTO option. For 1971 and beyond, engine output declined in the face of emission controls and, later, the fuel crunch. The 1968 bodyshell lasted through '72. After that, GTO again became a package option. The 455 Super Duty V8 with 310 bhp was still available for '74. The next year, GTO became an option for the compact Pontiac Ventura. No models after 1970 are really collectible now.

JOHN THOMSON
My Best Freind
who d did't make it
RK

This flag was presented to me on my return from Vietnam after spending 5 years as a prisoner of war. It represents to me a commitment of this nation to freedom and liberty; it represents a commitment of this nation to ensure the return of those lost or captured during time of war; it represents an appreciation the American people have for the sacrifices given by it's sons and daughters; and it represents to me a continued commitment we have to preserve the ideals we have fought for and pass on to our youth as they are the future of the United Stated of America, and the hope of the world.

The cross was made from a toothpaste tube and tie from my prison uniform. It represents the faith I had in God and country and it continues to represent the faith I have that the issue of those still missing will soon be resolved; that those still alive will be returned to their families for they have suffered more than we can know. I pray for them. I pray for their families, for the anguish of not knowing can only be greater than their loss. And I pray for the men and women that are gone and that some day we will be reunited on a higher plane, one in which we will no longer have to experience the pain, suffering and loss we are now required to preserve freedom. To you I salute.

Forever with us,

John G. Sparks

John G. Sparks

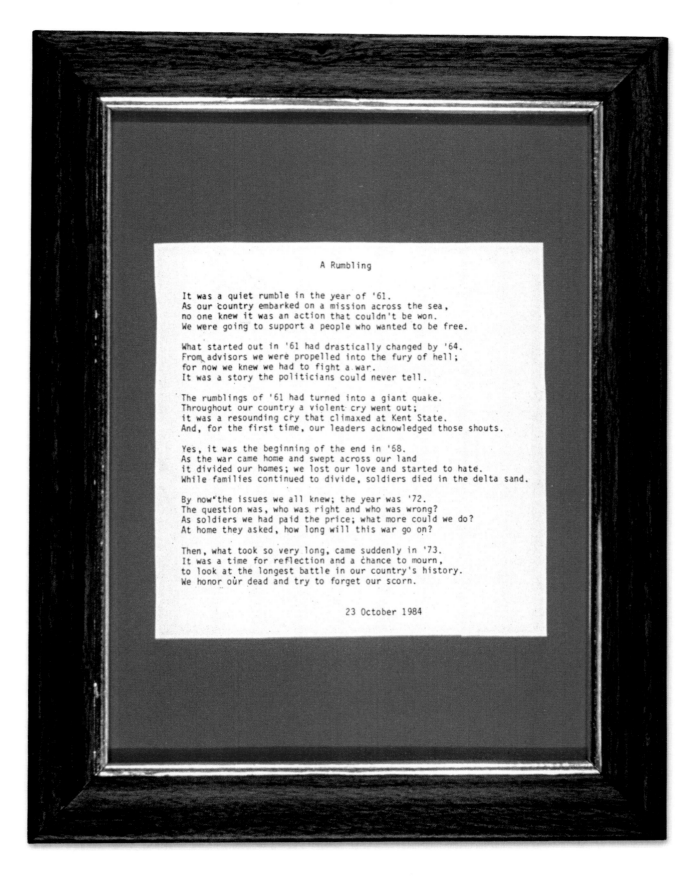

A Rumbling

It was a quiet rumble in the year of '61.
As our country embarked on a mission across the sea,
no one knew it was an action that couldn't be won.
We were going to support a people who wanted to be free.

What started out in '61 had drastically changed by '64.
From advisors we were propelled into the fury of hell;
for now we knew we had to fight a war.
It was a story the politicians could never tell.

The rumblings of '61 had turned into a giant quake.
Throughout our country a violent cry went out;
it was a resounding cry that climaxed at Kent State.
And, for the first time, our leaders acknowledged those shouts.

Yes, it was the beginning of the end in '68.
As the war came home and swept across our land
it divided our homes; we lost our love and started to hate.
While families continued to divide, soldiers died in the delta sand.

By now the issues we all knew; the year was '72.
The question was, who was right and who was wrong?
As soldiers we had paid the price; what more could we do?
At home they asked, how long will this war go on?

Then, what took so very long, came suddenly in '73.
It was a time for reflection and a chance to mourn,
to look at the longest battle in our country's history.
We honor our dead and try to forget our scorn.

23 October 1984

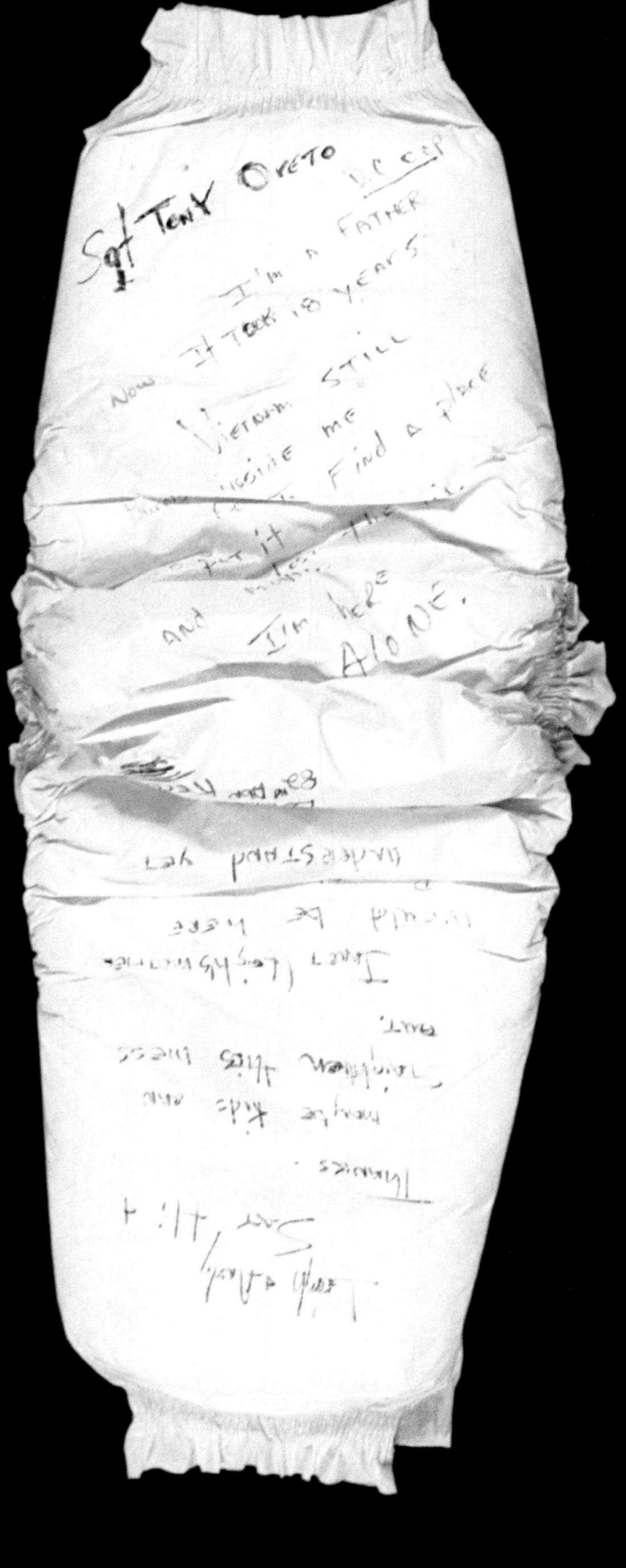
Sgt Tony Oveto
I'm a FATHER
It took 18 years
Now
Vietnam still
inside me
Find a place
I'm here
ALONE.
understand yet
be here
Thanks.

Though I never knew or could relate
the pain
I feel what you've been through
the strain
My heart goes out to you
I feel you near as I stand here
and gaze in wonder and
amazement that the
lifes were given to the struggle
and sacrife
So other people could try to
leave the poverty and pain
and lead a really normal
lives
Thank you so much I'll take
these memories with me always

Molly Estey
1995

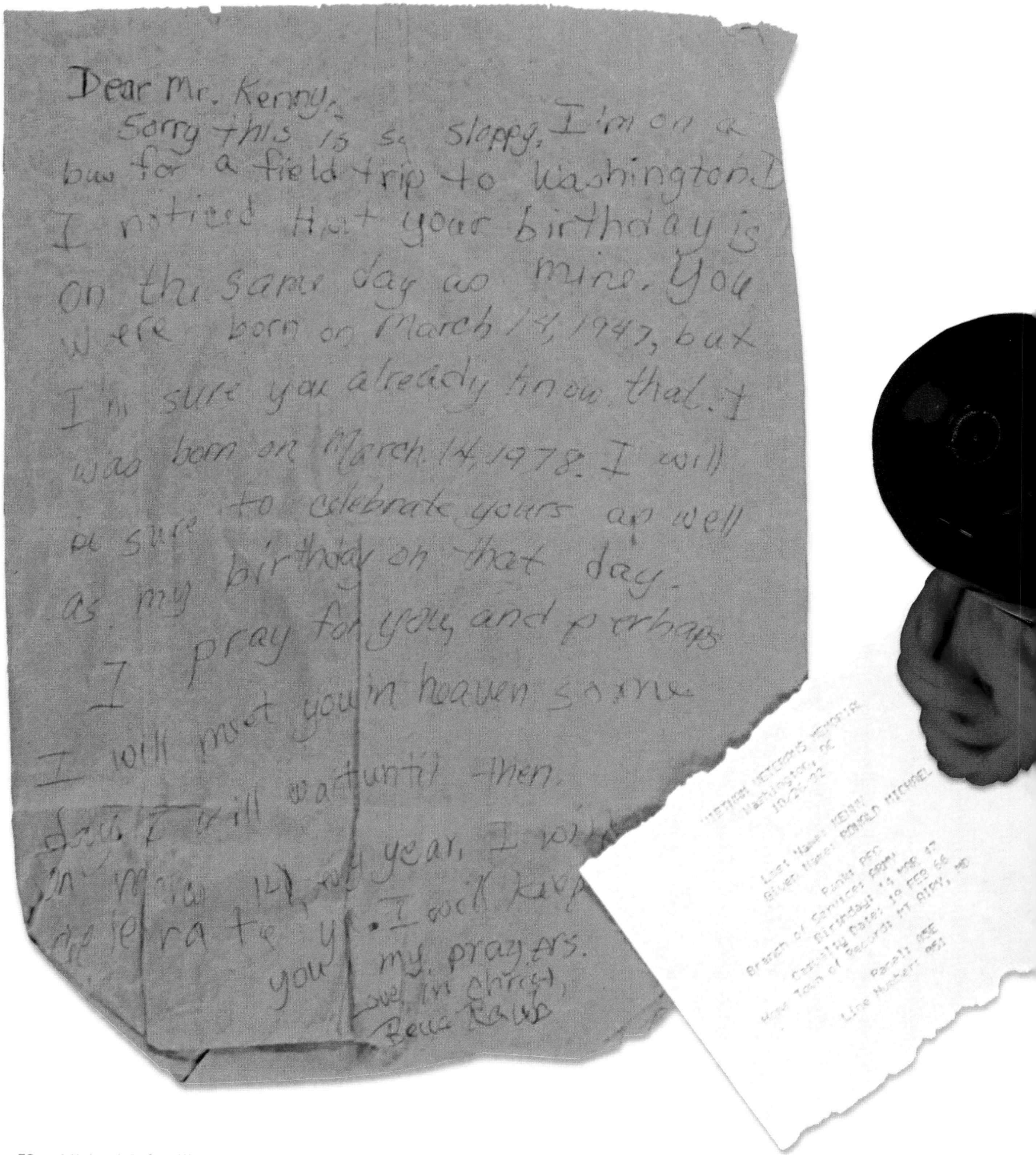

Dear Mr. Kenny,

Sorry this is so sloppy. I'm on a bus for a field trip to Washington. I noticed that your birthday is on the same day as mine. You were born on March 14, 1947, but I'm sure you already know that. I was born on March 14, 1978. I will be sure to celebrate yours as well as my birthday on that day.

I pray for you, and perhaps I will meet you in heaven someday. I will wait until then.

On March 14 next year, I will celebrate you. I will keep you in my prayers.

Love in Christ,
Becca Kaub

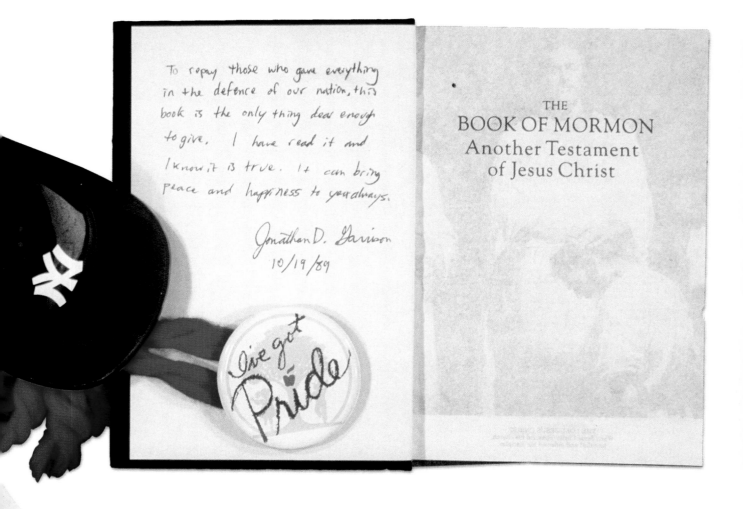

To repay those who gave everything in the defence of our nation, this book is the only thing dear enough to give. I have read it and I know it is true. It can bring peace and happiness to you always.

Jonathan D. Garrison
10/19/89

I've got Pride

THE
BOOK OF MORMON
Another Testament
of Jesus Christ

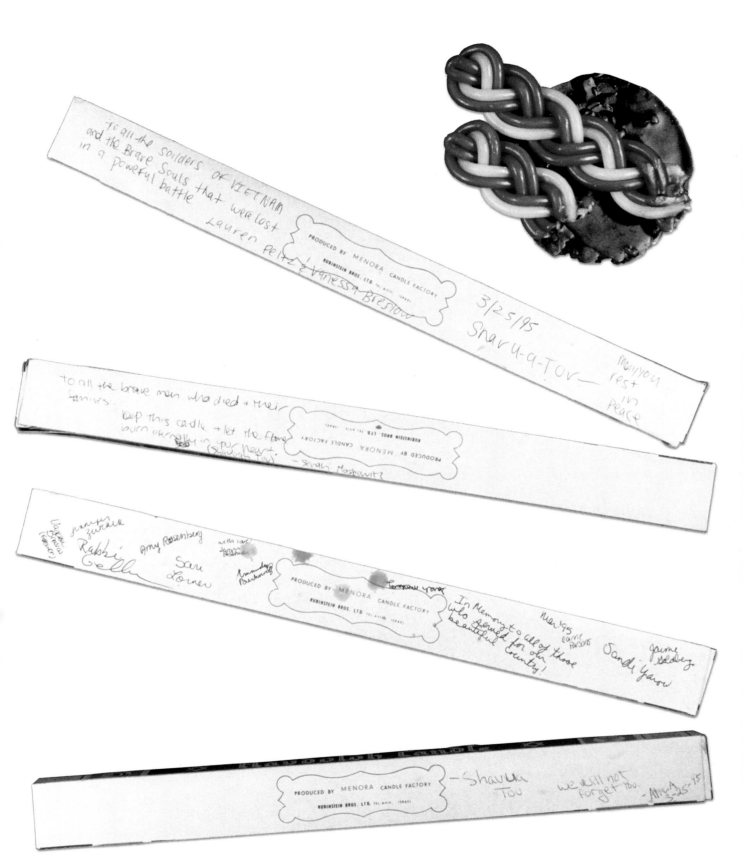

To all the soilders of VIETNAM and the Brave Souls that were lost in a powerful battle

Lauren Peltz & Vanessa Breslow

3/25/95

Shavu-a-Tov—

May you rest in Peace

to all the brave men who died + their families.

Keep this candle + let the flame burn eternally in your heart.

— Sarah Moskowitz

(Shavuah Tov)

Jennifer Zurkow

Vanessa Breslow (regards)

Amy Rosenberg

Rabbi Gellman

Sari Lerner

In Memory to all of those who served for our beautiful country!

Mar '95

Sandi Yarow

Jaime Goldberg

PRODUCED BY MENORA CANDLE FACTORY

RUBINSTEIN BROS. LTD. TEL AVIV. ISRAEL

— Shavua Tov

we will not forget you

— Amy A. 3-25-95

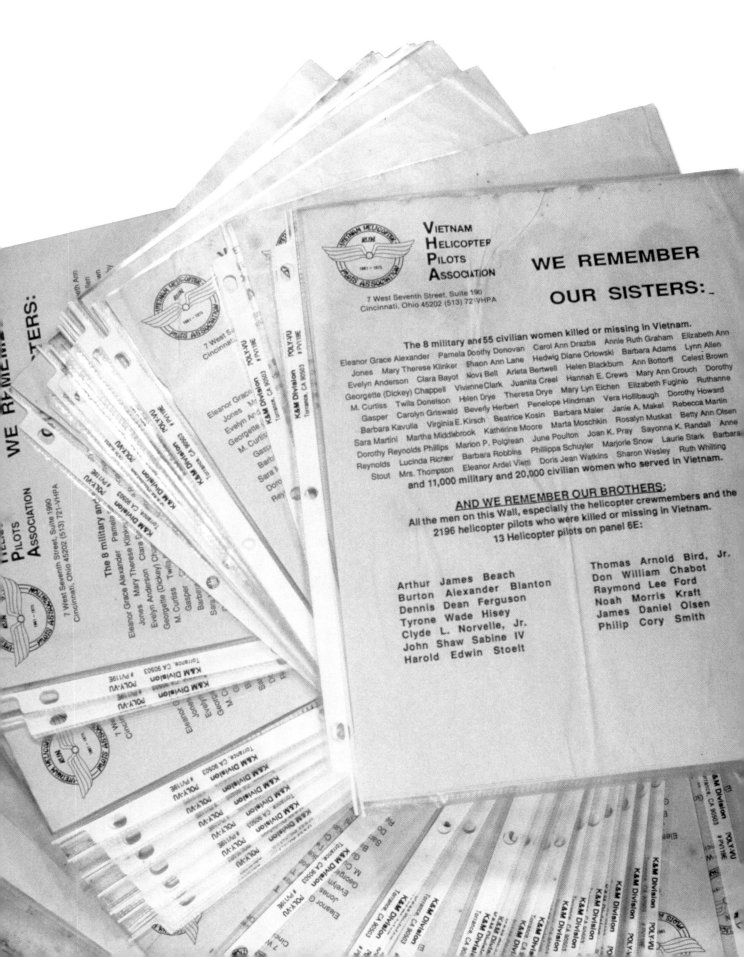

VIETNAM
HELICOPTER
PILOTS
ASSOCIATION

7 West Seventh Street, Suite 190
Cincinnati, Ohio 45202 (513) 721-VHPA

WE REMEMBER

OUR SISTERS:

The 8 military and 55 civilian women killed or missing in Vietnam.

Eleanor Grace Alexander Pamela Doothy Donovan Carol Ann Drazba Annie Ruth Graham Elizabeth Ann
Jones Mary Therese Klinker Shaon Ann Lane Hedwig Diane Orlowski Barbara Adams Lynn Allen
Evelyn Anderson Clara Bayot Nova Bell Arleta Bertwell Helen Blackburn Ann Bottorff Celest Brown
Georgette (Dickey) Chappell Vivanne Clark Juanita Creel Hannah E. Crews Mary Ann Crouch Dorothy
M. Curtiss Twila Donelson Helen Drye Theresa Drye Mary Lyn Eichen Elizabeth Fuginio Ruthanne
Gasper Carolyn Griswald Beverly Herbert Penelope Hindman Vera Hollibaugh Dorothy Howard
Barbara Kavulia Virginia E. Kirsch Beatrice Kosin Barbara Maler Janie A. Makel Rebecca Martin
Sara Martini Martha Middlebrook Katherine Moore Marta Moschkin Rosalyn Muskat Betty Ann Olsen
Dorothy Reynolds Phillips Marion P. Polgrean June Poulton Joan K. Pray Sayonna K. Randall Anne
Reynolds Lucinda Richter Barbara Robbins Phillippa Schuyler Marjorie Snow Laurie Stark Barbara
Stout Mrs. Thompson Eleanor Ardel Vietti Doris Jean Watkins Sharon Wesley Ruth Whitting

and 11,000 military and 20,000 civilian women who served in Vietnam.

AND WE REMEMBER OUR BROTHERS;

All the men on this Wall, especially the helicopter crewmembers and the
2196 helicopter pilots who were killed or missing in Vietnam.
13 Helicopter pilots on panel 6E:

Arthur   James   Beach
Burton   Alexander   Blanton
Dennis   Dean   Ferguson
Tyrone   Wade   Hisey
Clyde   L.   Norvelle,   Jr.
John   Shaw   Sabine   IV
Harold   Edwin   Stoelt

Thomas   Arnold   Bird,   Jr.
Don   William   Chabot
Raymond   Lee   Ford
Noah   Morris   Kraft
James   Daniel   Olsen
Philip   Cory   Smith

IN MEMORY of

Sgt. William J. Thornhill
N.y.

Given to Him By
Montgomery Chieftain
1968.

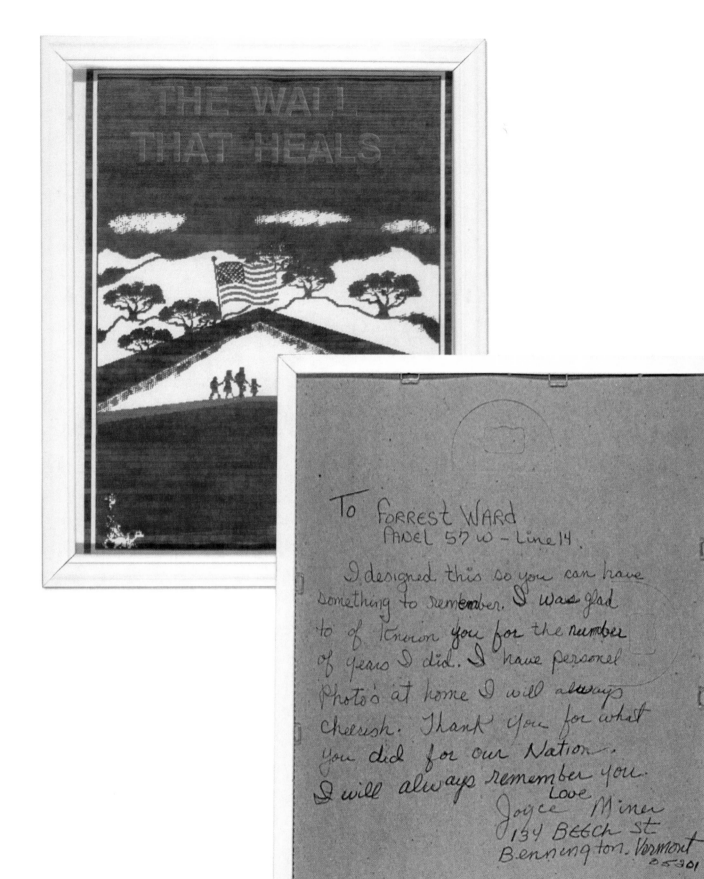

A small token of our deep appreciation

THIS SONG + sense of loss.
US FOR VETS To all vets, specially
remembering Hank DeHommel?

SIDE 1   Harold
DOLBY   Miller
Norm.   of the
                                            surviving
                                            vets of the
AUDIOMATRIX, TOLEDO, OH   V.V.H., Chap.
"30E 89"   35.

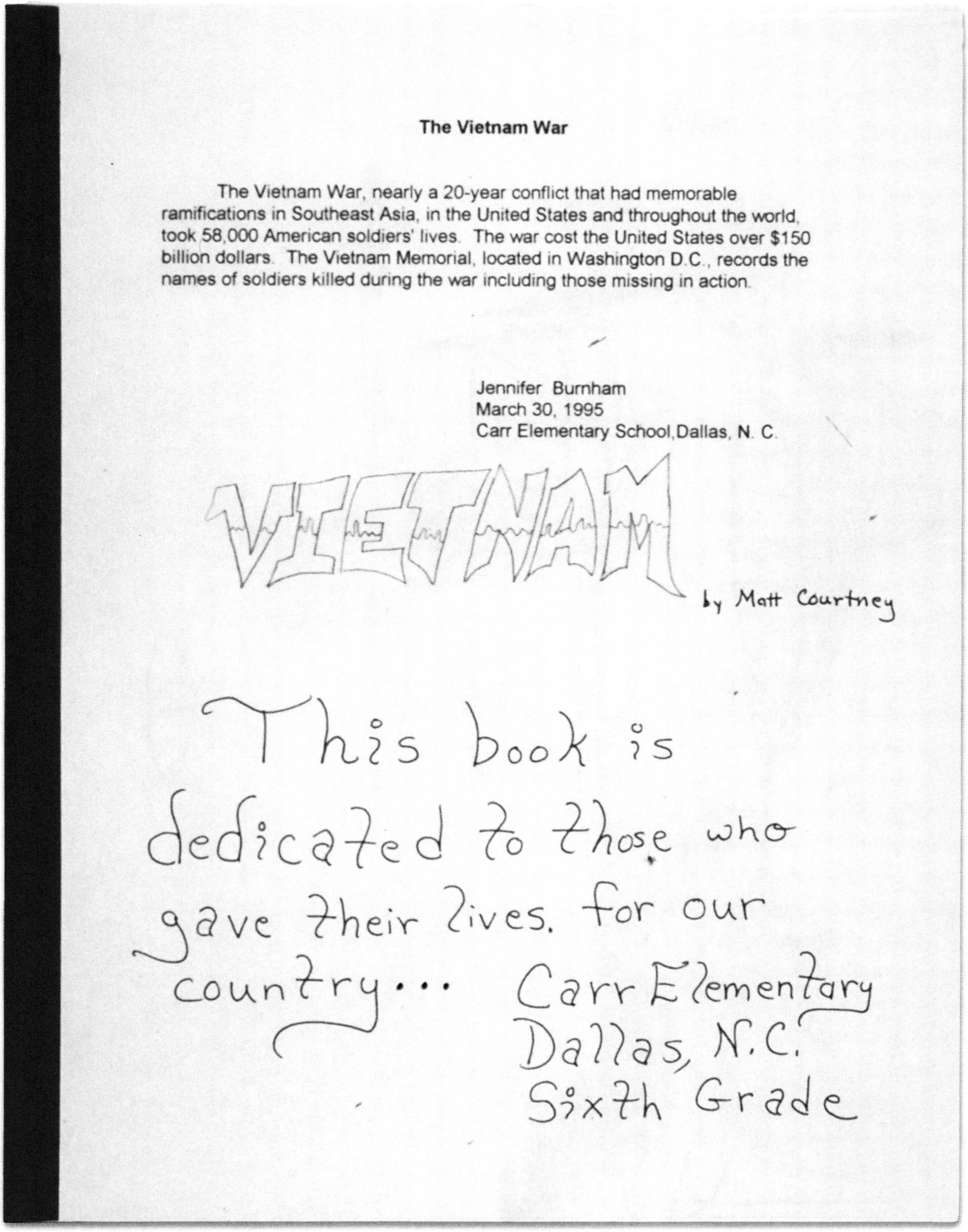

The Vietnam War

The Vietnam War, nearly a 20-year conflict that had memorable ramifications in Southeast Asia, in the United States and throughout the world, took 58,000 American soldiers' lives. The war cost the United States over $150 billion dollars. The Vietnam Memorial, located in Washington D.C., records the names of soldiers killed during the war including those missing in action.

Jennifer Burnham
March 30, 1995
Carr Elementary School, Dallas, N. C.

VIETNAM

by Matt Courtney

This book is dedicated to those who gave their lives. for our country... Carr Elementary Dallas, N.C. Sixth Grade

"Memorial Day"
May 30, 1868 - May 30, 1993
When flowers were placed on the
graves of the Union and Confederate Soldiers.

From the Soldiers of World War's One and Two.
To the dependents they left behind.
From the wars they never Counted.
To all the names that are on the wall.
From the accidents that just seem to happen.
To the questions that have no answers.

We hold you all in memory.
In our hearts and down the great hall.
God Bless all of our Armed Forces,
who's Soldier's died serving
our Country well.

To the men of the 199th ⟨CSM⟩
        I cared then,
        and now —
        and always!

    Kammy McCleery Malloy
                    APO 67-68
    Psalm 139:7-18   X-1506

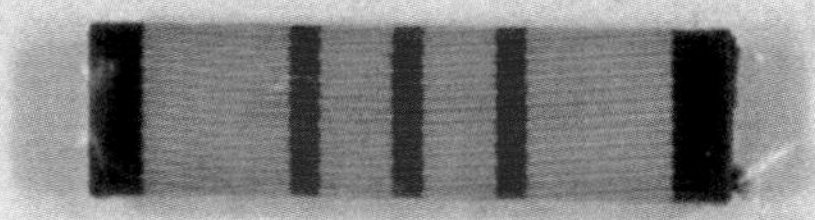

IF YOU WANT TO KNOW ABOUT
THE WOMEN AND HOW GOOD THEY
WERE, DON'T WASTE YOUR TIME
READING BOOKS.......
JUST ASK THE MEN.

Jeffrey S. Kanner
AUG. 5, 1994

JEFF KANNER
USMC VIETNAM
12/66 - 12/67

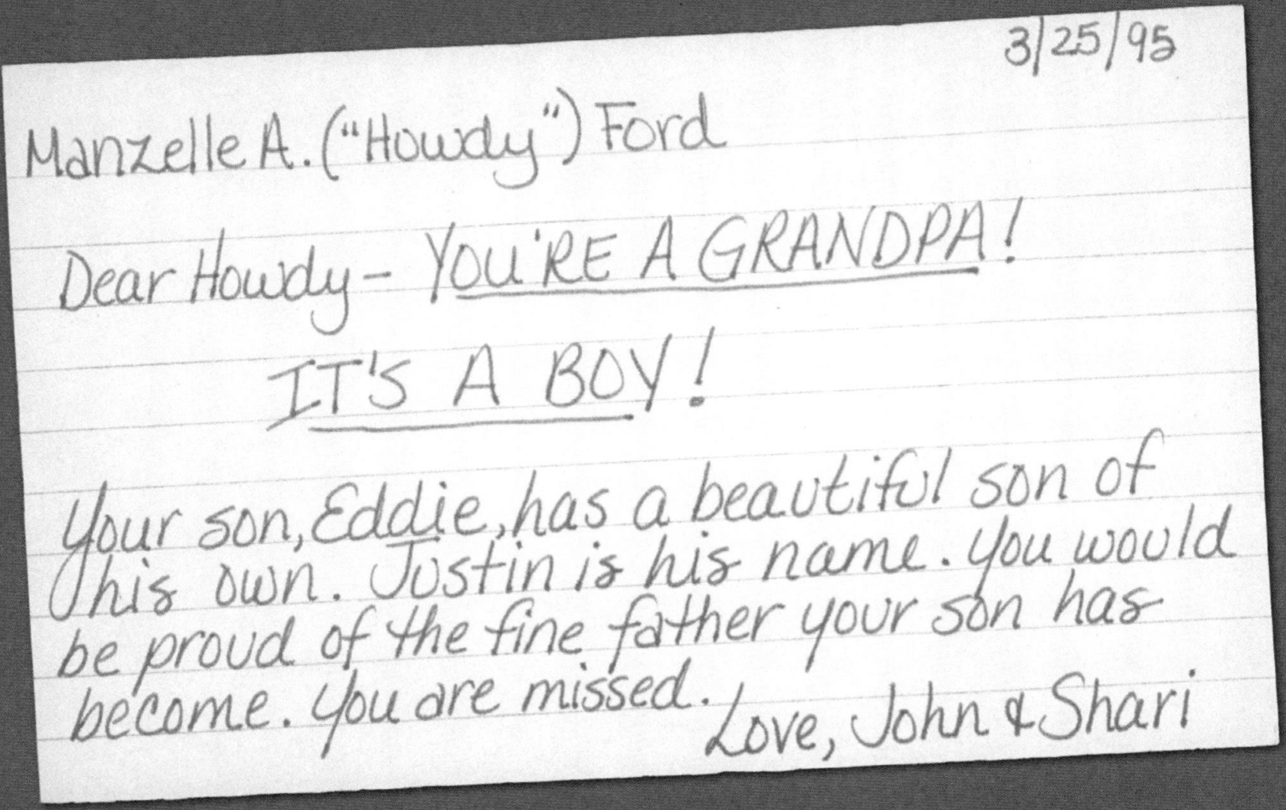

3/25/95

Manzelle A. ("Howdy") Ford

Dear Howdy — YOU'RE A GRANDPA!

IT'S A BOY!

Your son, Eddie, has a beautiful son of his own. Justin is his name. You would be proud of the fine father your son has become. You are missed. Love, John & Shari

june 21, 1988
This photo was taken at LZ [scribble]
uplift 1970 - 173rd Airbane
Brigade. My name is Kenneth
Calhoun, assigned to Co E 173rd.
The soldier in the photo was
nicknamed Ace and was from
Bronx, New York and was KIA
THIS IS MY 1ST VISIT TO THE WALL - THANKS
X-1287

Fill up the hole, piling dirt on top of the log cover and camouflaging it with sod. Make it look natural.

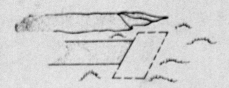

Then get in your hole and dig out a cace-like compartment under the cover.

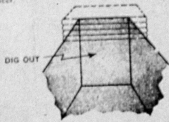

DIG OUT

Use the excavated dirt to add to and strengthen your parapet or your overhead cover. Excess dirt should be carefully carried away and hidden.

CONSTRUCTION
OF THE
TWO-MAN FOXHOLE

THE BASIC FIGHTING POSITION IS THE TWO-MAN FOX-HOLE. When you know how to build this position using the three tasks as a guide, you will then be able to quickly construct any fighting position. (See measurements below.)

After your squad leader has marked off your foxhole, told you where to dig and where your sector of fire is, QUICKLY PREPARE A HASTY POSITION and PARTIALLY CLEAR YOUR FIELDS OF FIRE. Dig deep enough to provide some protection and allow you to fire your weapon.

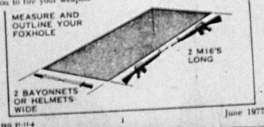

MEASURE AND OUTLINE YOUR FOXHOLE

2 M16'S LONG

2 BAYONNETS OR HELMETS WIDE

FM 21-11-4   1   June 1977

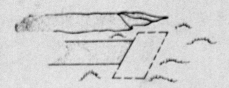

FOLLOW THESE STEPS FOR MORE PROTECTION

TASK 3   CONSTRUCT OVERHEAD COVER

After the basic foxhole is dug, you must create overhead cover as protection from indirect fires, the weather, and air observation. The way you build overhead cover depends on what material is on hand. Improvised cover support can be made from logs, planks, posts, broken sign boards, empty ammo boxes, debris from demolished buildings or anything rigid and strong enough to support a load of 18 inches or more earth.

To build overhead cover with expedient material, mark off an area at the side of your foxhole. Make it wider than the hole—wide enough to hold logs or planks which will support the cover (about 12 inches).

Dig this area out to a depth of about 18 inches, saving the soil for camouflage.

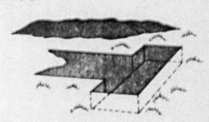

Next put supporting logs, planks, or whatever is available across the area to support the rest of the overhead cover material.

6   7

GENERAL ORDERS
NUMBER   4226

8 June 1967

AWARD OF THE SILVER STAR

1. TC 320. The following AWARD is announced posthumously.

PETERSEN, WILLIAM R   RIVATE FIRST CLASS E3 United States Army
Company A 1st Battalion 26th Infantry

Awarded: Silver Star
Date of action: 31 March 1967
Theater: Republic of Vietnam
Reason: For gallantry in action against a hostile force: On this
                date, Private First Class Petersen was moving with his
                company on a reconnaissance of the jungle surrounding
                a landing zone deep in War Zone C. The company was
                suddenly attacked by a large and well armed hostile force.
                Although it was evident that he and his comrades were
                outnumbered, Private First Class Petersen refused to
                withdraw. He placed effective fire into the insurgent
                ranks and encouraged his fellow soldiers to fight harder.
                Several times, the insurgent drives threatened to overrun
                the friendly positions. Each time, Private First Class
                Petersen moved to the area of heaviest fighting to assist
                his embattled comrades. After moments of fierce
                hand-to-hand combat, the repeated insurgent assaults
                were driven back. Private First Class Petersen succeeded
                in killing many Viet Cong before he was mortally wounded
                by hostile fire. His courageous actions motivated his
                comrades to stave off the insurgent onslaughts until
                friendly reinforcements arrived. Private First Class
                Petersen's unquestionable valor in close combat against
                numerically superior hostile forces is in keeping with
                the finest traditions of the military service and reflects
                great credit upon himself, the 1st Infantry Division, and
                the United States Army.
Authority: By direction of the President, as established by an Act of
                Congress 9 July 1918, and USARV Message 16695, dated
                1 July 1966.

        FOR THE COMMANDER:

OFFICIAL: EDWARD B. KIT
                                    Colonel, GS
                                    Chief of Staff

ALAN H. BADINE
Captain, AGC
Assistant Adjutant General

T.L. Smith
William Prather
1967-68
B Co.
3rd Bat
187th Abn In
101st Abn

I came he
Mike Kondor
You see
was after
his tru
knew
You kn
ta
to
tha
nev

Way Dad
July Flag
still do chan
Dan, we all ap

This basket fo
Prather (1967-68 B Co
Abn. Div.) have unselfish.

The two red flowers were given to Mike's mother and
father when he returned home to the states–safely.

The white bow is for his first born. His little girl
showed him that innocence and purity do exist in the world.

The blue rattle is for his boy. The next Kondor to
carry on the family name...and the honor that he
desperately worked so hard to defend.

The 2 wine glasses are for the 25th Wedding
Anniversary that he and his wife shall soon celebrate.
Proving to him that love can withstand any obstacles.

And the United States flag is for the eternal love,
prayer, and patriotism to these men who gave their life in
order for him to live.

...n Hoa Marines Strike
...Rich During Action

By Lt. Dave Richert

AN HOA—Marines of the 3rd Marine Regt. are "striking it rich" in the mountains west of An Hoa. During their first week of operation in this rugged territory they turned up a great array and quantity of North Vietnamese Army weapons and equipment.

A patrol from the regiment uncovered a weapons cache and hospital complex, the largest find thus far. Included were 11 weapons, a new mortar tube with accessory equipment, 150 packs, new clothing and about 100 lbs. of assorted documents.

"We saw a well used trail," explained Cpl. Mike Conroy, a scout, "and it led to this base area which showed signs of activity in the last 48 hours." He said it looked as if the area was built to accommodate about 50 persons.

Also in this complex a printing press and typewriter were uncovered, with propaganda and administrative material still on the rollers.

It is believed by some officials of the 3rd Marines that this area is an NVA group headquarters. "You find items like presses, training facilities, and POW compounds in base areas," says one. He further backs up his belief (Continued on Back Page)

An Hoa...

(Continued From Page 1) lief with the kill of a confirmed NVA "engineer" and capture of numerous regiments, books, as well as the capture of two radios and an NVA who said he was a communicator. These people and items are usually found in rear areas.

The documents have come in such abundance and so rapidly that it will be several days before the full significance can be determined. There is little doubt, however, that Task Force Yankee has picked the right arm for Operation Taylor Common.

Other Marine units participating in the operation have made similar significant finds. These include a Russian anti-aircraft gun, a training complex and messhall with facilities for 100, and a POW camp, where, according to Conroy, wood smoke and heat was still detectable.

Spark...

(Continued From Page 1) Common when he was killed. He was one of the youngest regimental commanders in the Marine Corps.

Seven others aboard the helicopter died with Col. Spark—three Marines and four Army men. The three other Marines were: LtCol. Ermil Lee Whisman, commanding officer, 1st Bn., 12th Marines; SgtMaj. Ted E. McClintock, sergeant major of the 3rd Marines; and LCpl. Frederick Daniel Kansik, a radioman with Headquarters Co., 3rd Marines.

Col. Spark, a 22-year Marine veteran, had directed an assault against heavily fortified enemy positions and had boarded the helicopter to better observe and control the operation in the mountainous jungle terrain.

The helicopter was hit by enemy fire and crashed into the jungle.

Col. Spark was born June 9, 1927 in New York City. After graduating from Dartmouth College with a bachelor of arts degree in history he was commissioned a second lieutenant in the Marine Corps in 1946.

Before arriving in Vietnam in March 1968, Col. Spark served as the Marine aide to the Undersecretary of the Navy. He was assistant chief of staff, G-2, 3rd Marine Division, before assuming command of the 3rd Marines in November.

He is survived by his wife, Mrs. Eleanor Marie Spark, and three children living in Alexandria, Va.

LtCol. Whisman was born in Winchester, Ky., and served in the U.S. Air Force prior to being commissioned a second lieutenant in the Marine Corps in 1951.

He began his Vietnam tour last August. His wife, Mrs. Loyse B. Whisman and four children live in Wichita Falls, Texas.

SgtMaj. McClintock was born Jan. 22, 1919, in Seattle, Wash., and entered the Marine Corps in 1943. He was due to rotate back to the United States this month after 13 months overseas.

Col. Michael M. Spark

Col. Spark Killed In Helo Crash

DA NANG—Col. Michael Melvin Spark, commanding officer of the 3rd Marines, 3rd Marine Division, was killed Jan. 15 while directing his troops from a command helicopter, an Army UH-1E, which was shot down by enemy automatic weapons fire 14 miles southwest of An Hoa.

Col. Spark, a native of New York City, was commanding his regiment in Operation Taylor (Continued on Back Page)

Joint Operation Finds Enemy Supply Caches

Sgt. Mike Stokey

AN HOA—During the first 22 days of Operation Taylor Common, a joint multi-battalion search-and-clear operation in the An Hoa basin, six Marine battalions and three battalions from the 1st Army of the Republic of Vietnam (ARVN) Ranger Group accounted for 596 North Vietnamese and 170 Viet Cong Kills.

The multi-battalion operation, conducted by Leathernecks of the 3rd, 5th and 7th Marine Regiments, also has uncovered scores of NVA and VC complexes and unearthed tons of enemy supplies. Taylor Common began on Dec. 7.

As the Leathernecks began sweeping through the mountainous region, they accounted for 171 of the enemy killed — 102 NVA and 69 VC, as of Dec. 18. ARVN figures for that period showed 161 enemy killed — 72 NVA and 29 VC.

Among the miscellaneous gear unearthed were 227 enemy packs, 83 gas masks, 100 gallons of kerosene, 200 pounds of corn and 99.8 tons of rice.

Captured ammunition includes (Continued on Back Page)

Joint Operation...

(Continued From Page 1) 125 mortars, 103 grenades, 127 rifles, 20 crew-served weapons, 3 tactical field radios and 20,468 small arms rounds.

Some 68 enemy complexes have been destroyed by the allied force, including 414 bunkers, 123 huts, 13 NVA headquarter sites, one prison, one hospital and four aid stations.

One find was made by elements of the 5th Marines as they uncovered a large NVA base camp Dec. 20, consisting of more than 50 huts with attached bunkers. A graveyard was also uncovered in the complex containing 35 enemy bodies.

Recently, a patrol from the 3rd Marines uncovered a sizable weapons cache and hospital complex including about 100 pounds of assorted documents. Included in the complex, was a printing press and typewriter with propaganda and administrative material still on the rollers.

Other Marine units participating in the operation have made

similar significant finds. These include a Russian anti-aircraft gun, a training complex and messhall with facilities for 100, and a POW camp.

Going into the 22nd day of the operation, Marines accounted for 298 of the enemy killed...173 NVA and 125 VC with 96 listed as detainees; 71 individual and 5 crew-served weapons were captured.

ARVN figures, as of Dec. 29 include 468 enemy killed...423 NVA and 45 VC with 86 detainees; 89 individual and 20 crew-served weapons were captured.

The operation is still in its early stage, and is aimed at uprooting the enemy and destroying refuge sites and command posts near the Laotian border.

Col. SPARK
Sgt. Maj. McCLINTOCK
Cpl. KANSIK

YOU ARE MORE THAN JUST NAMES ON
"THE WALL".
WE BELIEVED IN A NOBLE CAUSE.
I WAS UNABLE TO MOURN YOU THEN.
I MOURN YOU NOW.
REST IN PEACE.
Cpl. A. Cole   Headquarters Co.
3rd Marine Regt.

THE UNIVERSITY OF RHODE ISLAND
ARMY ROTC
"CRAMER'S SABERS BATTALION"

HONORS

PARKER D. CRAMER, CLASS OF 1959
ROBERT L. MOSHER, CLASS OF 1959
HENRY R. PHILLIPS, CLASS OF 1962
CARL W. MYLLYMAKI, III, CLASS OF 1965
CARMEN DeCUBELLIS, JR., CLASS OF 1968

WHO GAVE THEIR LIVES
IN THE SERVICE OF THEIR NATION

Avery Macleod, Cadet Lieutenant Colonel
Battalion Commander

Robert McGowan, Major
Professor of Military Science

"FSM"

A grey December dusk it was twenty years ago -
A large crowd stood listening on campus outside Wheeler Hall
        to loudspeakers ...   on the steps:
The Academic Senate of the Berkeley faculty
        was debating support for the
        Free Speech Movement
Students marched for the right to speak on campus
        opinions perhaps unpopular -
        in essence, a Hyde Park forum.
The tense and silent crowd burst into cheers
        when the Senate vote was announced:
More than 900 of the faculty pushed history
        by voting support eight to one
        for a student's right to advocacy.
The cause of a semester of turmoil won legitimacy,
        even in the San Francisco Examiner,
        and shoved toward the White House
        a "B" movie actor.
Tonight, 20 years almost to the hour ...
        student conduct to this day is judged by the University
        according to rules won, not authoritarian caprice.
Another American Revolution was granted "Godspeed!"

                                    Concord, California
                                    December 8, 1984

+ + + + : : : : + + + + + + +

the
YOSEMITE
GROUP

Box 386
San Francisco
94101

X-2132

THE ORDER OF THE MEMORIAL SERVICE

THE HYMN OF TRUST
God of our fathers, whose almighty hand
Leads forth in beauty all the starry band
Of shining worlds in splendor through the skies,
Our greateful songs before Thy throne arise

From war's alarms, from deadly pestilence,
Be Thy strong arm our ever sure defense;
Thy true religion in our hearts increase,
Thy bounteous goodness nourish us in peace

Refresh Thy people on their toilsome way,
Lead us from night to never ending day;
Fill all our lives with love and grace divine,
And glory, loud, and praise be ever Thine.

THE INVOCATION
   C: In the Name of the Father and of the + Son
      And of the Holy Spirit.   P: AMEN

THE INTROIT (all)
Our help is in the Name of the Lord
Who made heaven and earth.

Like as a father pitieth his children, so the Lord
Pietieth them that fear Him. For He knows our frame;
He remembereth that we are dust.

I am the Resurrection and the Life; he that believeth
In Me, though He were dead, yet shall he live; and
Whosoever liveth and believeth in Me shall never die.

I heard a voice from heaven saying unto me: Write,
Blessed are the dead which die in the Lord from
Henceforth; yea, saith the Spirit, that they may rest
from their labors; and their works do follow them.

THE GLORIA PATRI (all)
Glory be to the Father and to the Son and to the
Holy Spirit, as it was in the begenning is now and
ever shall be, world without ent. Amen.

THE KYRIE (responsively)
C: Lord be kind to us
P: LORD BE KIND TO US
C: Christ be good to us
P: CHRIST BE GOOD TO US
C: Lord be very kind to us
P: LORD BE VERY KIND TO US
C: Christ be very good to us
P: CHRIST BE VERY GOOD TO US
C: Lord have mercy upon us.

THE PSALM

THE LESSON

THE COMMEMORATION

THE LITANY OF COMMEMORATION
(responsively from the inse

THE PRAYER OF OUR LORD (all, s

THE MARINE HYMN
Eternal Father grant we p
To all Marines both night
The courage, honor, stren
Their land to serve Thy
Be Thou the shield forev
From every peril to the

Lord guard and guide th
Through the great space
Be with them always in
In darkening storms or
O hear us when we lift
For those in peril in

THE BENEDICTION

TAPS

Richard B Fox

Margaret Murawskas

~~Ben Strong~~

Laura Allocco Abstar

Dee Rivers

Phillip Furao

Shirley Breialing

Marie Natividad

~~(VL) Alice~~

Alice Kono

Wendy Klaufisch

Patricia Olson

"Emily Tolega-Toelu"

Nita Fragas

Richard Kaneko

Jeanne Fukiji

Anna Marie O Beto

Lorraine Tollya Dolar

"Kevin" Monaghan
"Melodi Downing"
Mike Henky

William Ellis *

Becky L. Schirka "

Ralph Harrison Dwight

(CMD 381h Charlie company commander)

Dustin F. D——

Howard Wissman

C/KCDR Craig W Long

B—— Ra—— LCDR

Radford High
School
Honolulu,
Hawaii

THIS FLAG IS IN
HONOR OF THE MEMORY
OF LIEUTENNANT
COMMANDER RICHARD
MINNICH, JUNIOR, WHO
WAS REPORTED MISSING IN
ACTION.
I NEVER KNEW HIM
BUT I WORE A BRACELET
ENGRAVED WITH HIS NAME FOR
5 YEARS. I WILL ALWAYS
REMEMBER HIM. SOMEDAY, I WILL
RETURN AND LEAVE THE BRACELET.

SANDY
PHILADELPHIA, PA

UNCLASSIFIED

(Classification)

UNIT OR SECTION
3d Battalion, 9th Marines
PLACE
Camp CARROLL, RVN

FROM (Date and hour)	TO (Date and hour)
300001	302400H March 1967

TIME		SERIAL NO.	DATE TIME GROUP	INCIDENTS, MESSAGES, ORDERS	ACTION TAKEN
IN	OUT				M—Maps T—Troops / S—Staff F—File
0600		1	300530	Received weather report from 3d Marines	SF
1000		2	301000	Chopped OPCON of Company E 2/26 to parent unit.	SF 3d Marines
1030		3	301030	Company M advance platoon commenced day's activities in assigned area of operation.	SF 3d Marines
1100		4	301100	Received intelligence report from 3d Marines	SF
1145		5	301140	Company I found two decomposed NVA bodies while patrolling in assigned area of operation. One was dressed in khaki and the other was dressed in black. There was no type of identification and there were no documents found in the area.	SF 3d Marines
1300		6	301300	Company M and Command Group commenced move to begin days activities in assigned area of operation in accordance with Operation Overlay 1-67.	SF 3d Marines
1530		7	301535	Company M lead elment platoon made contact with estimated 6 NVA YD 114656. The NVS were sitting in ambush and were spotted by Company M. The platoon assaulted the ambush killing 1 NVA. Unit pursuing the rest of the NVA were told to be careful of a VC ambush. 1 NVA was killed in pursuit and the pursuit ended when the remaining NVA appeared to enter the village complex. Two NVA KIA CONF, two automatic rifles, one automatic pistol, 4 ChiCom grnades, 6 30 round banana clips, 2 packs and one e-tool captured. Two USMC WIA medevaced.	SF 3d Marines
1800		8	1800	Company I began receiving incoming mortar fire YD 096652. I-2, 3, 4, and CP were hit with heavy 60mm mortr fire and S/A fire. The enemy advanced to friendly positions under the morter fire and hit the units after lifting of the mortars. The enemy infiltrated friendly positions with friendly units suffering casualties 16 KIA, 52 WIA, 62 NVA KIA CONF 2 NVA Captured.	

(See reverse side for instructions)

PAGE NO
1

CONFIDENTIAL

ENCLOSURE ( )

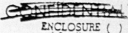

To you from failing hands we throw
the torch; be it yours to hold high
If ye break faith with us who die
We shall not sleep, though poppies grow
In Flanders Field.

We can only hope & pray
that one day this nation
will fully realize the total
injustice & abandonment of
all the POW's & MIA's.
How much longer can the lie
go on? Are people really that
blind, that they just don't see?

Great is the Nation who
Has Heroes
Poor is the Nation who
Having them forgets!

3/30/86

May His presence
fill your heart
with hope,
and bring you
lasting peace
and joy.

Happy Easter, Father
God Bless You Always

Daddy.
We love you
& we miss you,
GARY SR., HEIDI, Amanda,
ANDREA, & GARY III

Inside the document on the flag:

THE FLAG
OF THE
UNITED STATES
OF AMERICA

This is to certify that the accompanying flag was flown
over the United States Capitol on May 1, 1987,
at the request of the Honorable Peter H. Kostmayer,
Member of Congress.

This flag will be used at the Vietnam Veterans' Memorial
at the request of Jorge de Dios.

TO ALL OUR COMRADES
WHO GAVE UP SO MUCH.
THIS BALL IS SIGNED BY
THOSE WHO SERVED

KANSAS CITY
SECTIONAL AERONAUTICAL CHART
SCALE 1:500,000

Lambert Conformal Conic Projection Standard Parallels 33°20' and 38°40'
Topographic data corrected to April 1971

6 TH EDITION corrected to include airspace amendments effective **July 22, 1971**
and all other aeronautical data received by June 21, 1971
Consult appropriate NOTAMS and Flight Information
Publications for supplemental data and current information.
This chart will become OBSOLETE FOR USE IN NAVIGATION upon publication of
the next edition scheduled for JAN. 6, 1972

PUBLISHED IN ACCORDANCE WITH INTER-AGENCY AIR CARTOGRAPHIC COMMITTEE
SPECIFICATIONS AND AGREEMENTS. APPROVED BY:
DEPARTMENT OF DEFENSE FEDERAL AVIATION ADMINISTRATION DEPARTMENT OF COMMERCE

CONTOUR INTERVAL
500 feet
Intermediate contours shown at 250 feet

——— 500 ———   ——— 250 ———
· Basic   Intermediate

HIGHEST TERRAIN elevation is
2430 feet
located at 36°05'N – 93°22'W

Critical elevation - - - , - - - - - - - - - - - .4254
Approximate elevation - - - - - - - - - - - ×3200
Doubtful locations are indicated by omission
of the point locator (dot or "x") .

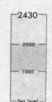

MAXIMUM TERRAIN ELEVATIONS
Maximum Terrain elevation figures, centered in the area completely bounded by ticked
lines of latitude and longitude, are represented in THOUSANDS and HUNDREDS of feet
BUT DO NOT INCLUDE ELEVATIONS OF VERTICAL OBSTRUCTIONS.

3100 feet - - - - - - - - - 3¹

CONVERSION OF ELEVATIONS
FEET 0 2 4 6 8 10 12 14 16 18 20 22 24 26 28 30
(Thousands)
METERS 0 1 2 3 4 5 6 7 8 9
(Thousands)
Published at Washington, D.C.
U.S. Department of Commerce
National Oceanic and Atmospheric Administration
National Ocean Survey

PRICE 80 CENTS

Michael Sofarelli

Bless Those Who
Serve Their Country

TO: Michael, O'Tate
From: Paul W. Allen

Michael, I refused
to believe it would. In
though reality of death
in Vietnam died became
a reality. I really find
it hard to say what Ian
going to say. The reality
of things hurt. And still
do. reality sent me
back to the world with
a to of fuel Memories
they are still with me
I think only of the
good times we had there
I know you would want
it that way

THE COLLECTOR'S SERIES
by Silberne
DISTINCTIVE PRINTS FOR FRAMING

Dear Ralph
Brower

My name is Matt Mirmak,
My dad, Ed Mirmak was in
the Air Force w/ you. My
dad never got to thank you
for keeping him in the service.
He thanks you with all love

sincerely
Matt Mirmak
son of Maj Edward
J Mirmak USAF

W3081

WASHINGTON, D. C.

CS-13

PUBLISHED BY SILBERNE SOUVENIR SALES, INC., WASHINGTON, D. C. 20018

Though you might be as quiet as
the pools of paradise, but you
all know that, you are not forgotten.
Because you are too young to
fall sleep for-ever.
So is the great Earth.

19-Jun.90 Peter

Proclamation

Whereas, the Governing Body of the Borough of Fort Lee has designated the first week in June 1985 as Viet Nam Veterans' Recognition Week; and

Whereas, thousands of our youth gave the supreme sacrifice, while many thousands more were wounded and missing in action; and

Whereas, the purpose of this designation is to recognize and pay tribute to those Americans who fought and served in the Viet Nam conflict and because participation in such conflict was so unpopular as to cause such divisiveness in this country that our returning servicemen and women were greeted with indifference, if not outright hostility.

Now, therefore, be it resolved that I, Nicholas Corbiscello, Mayor of the Borough of Fort Lee, in the County of Bergen, State of New Jersey, do hereby proclaim the first week in June 1985 Viet Nam Veterans' Recognition Week, and urge everyone able to do so to observe this week and remember the devotion and sacrifice of the young men and women who answered their nation's call.

Nicholas Corbiscello, Mayor

Attest:

Carol Kohout, Borough Clerk

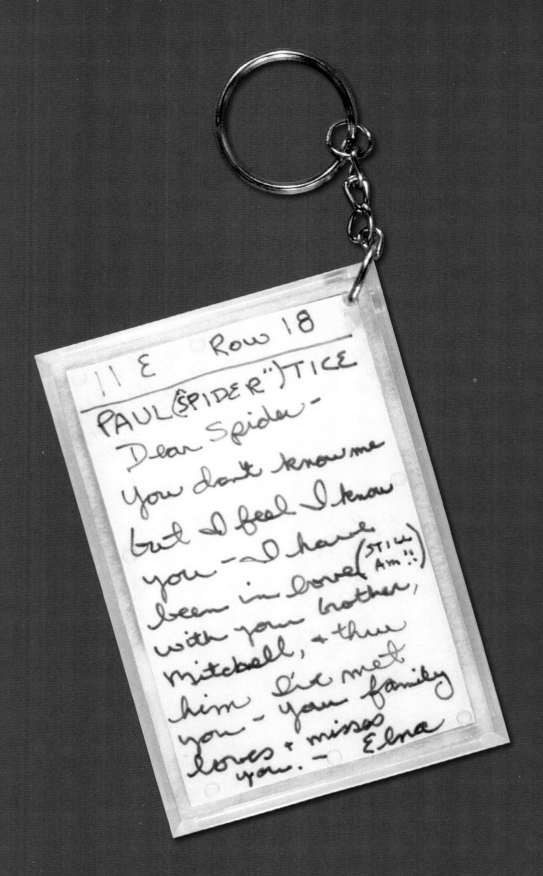

11 E   Row 18

PAUL (ŜPIDER") TICE

Dear Spider –

You don't know me
but I feel I know
you – I have (STILL AM!!)
been in love
with your brother,
Mitchell, + thru
him I've met
you – your family
loves + misses
you. – Elna

I saw an eagle in a dream
His mouth was opened in a silent scream.
His wings were torn, from his struggle there.
His feathers worn, from his pain and despair.
He looked toward Heaven as if to pray,
God, I want to be free today!
Free, to fly in your heavens above.
Free to feel my country's love.
He struggled there and no one came
to release his leg from his captors' chain.
He was abandoned after the war.
He doesn't even look for help anymore.
I even saw people in that horrible scene,
Unwilling to answer the eagle's scream.
It's been fifteen years and his agony grows
Someone have mercy, and Let Him Go!

Dear Jim,

    I was only sixteen when you died. I'm
sorry I didn't write to you when you were in
Viet Nam. I guess I was to busy just being a
kid!
    You asked me to look after your kids the
day you left. I did the best I could at the
time, I was so young. I cried when you died.
I thought of you often as I grew up.
    I went to Viet Nam myself, three years
after you. I never said this to you while
you were alive, but I love you and I miss you
very much. I think of you almost every day.
I miss you calling me "Little Brother".
    I'm sorry I didn't come here sooner: I
just wasn't ready. I'm stronger now, I think
I can handle it.
    Did you know you're a grandpa now?
    Take care "Big Brother" some day you can
call me "Littler Brother" again.

    Love always,

    Danny

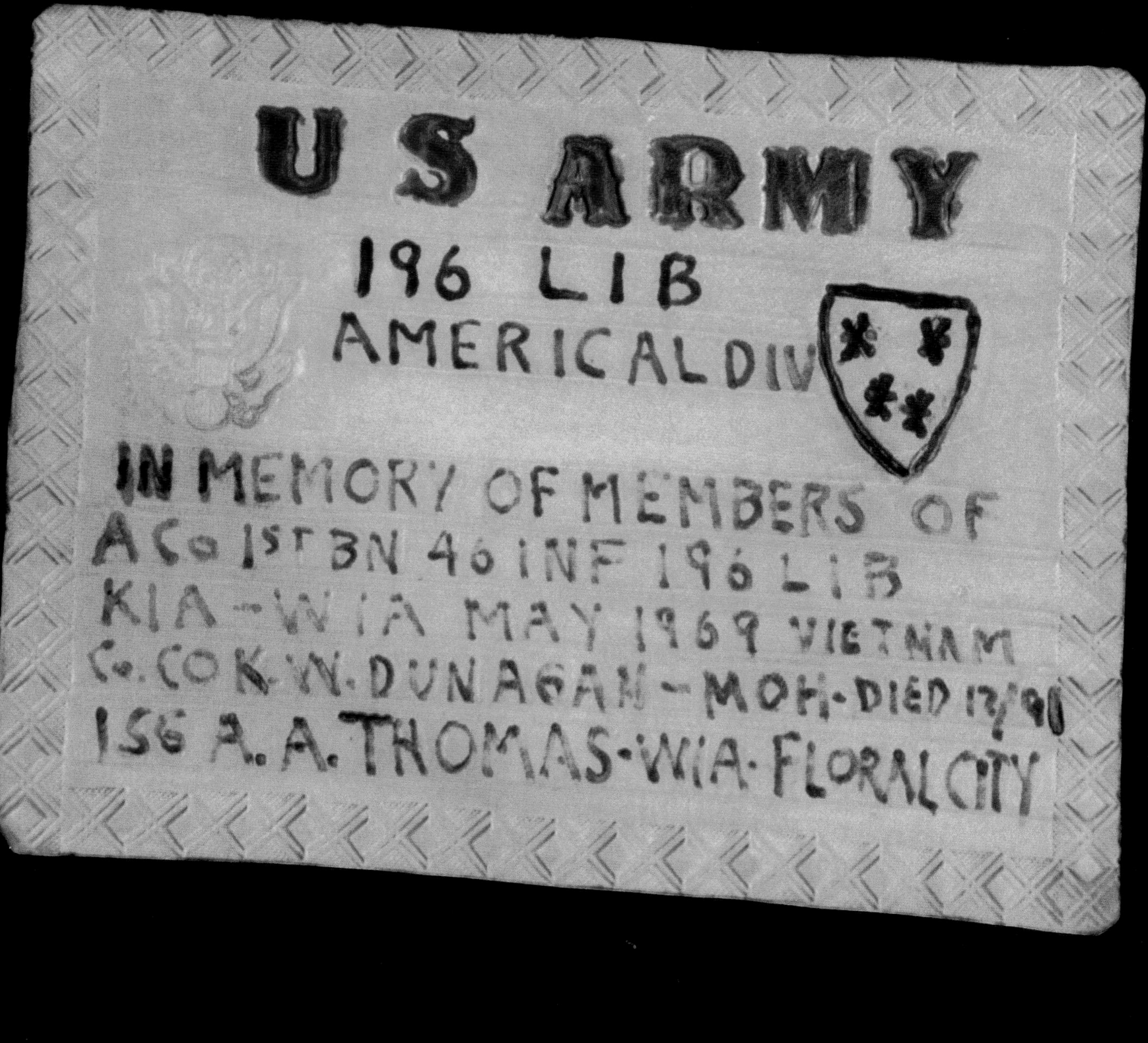

US ARMY
196 LIB
AMERICAL DIV

IN MEMORY OF MEMBERS OF
A Co 1ST BN 46 INF 196 LIB
KIA - WIA MAY 1969 VIETNAM
Co. CO K. W. DUNAGAN - MOH - DIED 12/90
1SG A. A. THOMAS - WIA - FLORAL CITY

Bill

Dear Bill,
It's been 19 years since
you were killed. I will
see your name today.

I am leaving this
letter and the phone
you gave me so many
years ago.

I'm happy, I have
Mark and have four
wonderful girls. You
would like them.

Rest in Peace Bill
I Love You
Your,
Sue

Desert Thoughts

In
mEMory
OF
Aaron Howard (Pfc)
&
Dodge Powell (Sgt)

It's only just beginning,
The end nowhere in sight.
But not knowing is the worst thing'
Will it end or will we fight?

A madman as a ruler,
With ego,greed and power,
He can't succeed,he must be stopped,
It's almost zero hour.

I knuckle down and ponder,
I bow my head and pray.
The one question that is paramount,
Is there peace today?

My thoughts already wander,
To things I call my own.
My wife,my friends,my fami
And the comforts of my hom

Much I wonder is unanswer
So I try to find out``Why?''
But if I must,yes,I'll fight,
And if I must....I'll die

Defending freedom is my mission,
And I've answered,every call.
I'll fight in heart and dust and sand,
And the dragon,he will fall

For I am called``American,''
And I say it clear and loud.
Not only am I strong and brave,
I'm the best....and I'm damn proud!!

Sgt. Dodge Powell (died shortly after this poem in Operation Desert Storm1990)

Always Remembering of
Scott A. Panfil
82nd Engr

Audentes Fortuna Juvat

the BEAR FLAG

NEWS

5¢

February 28, 1985   On The Road   Vol. IX, No. 2

E24

The Vietnam Veterans Memorial

In San Jose

    a half size replica of the Capital' Memorial ...

I came to the Rose Garden here

    with my friend in the rain

    and left him be to ponder the memory

    at a distance under a redwood.

Among the 58,000 names

    with help I found Carey's –

    white names on black glass ...

Casualty, August 2, 1967,

    Collinsville, Alabama – Captain, Air Force

I walked down the railway tracks with Carey

    after Sunday school for dinner with his family

We were each nine and classmates   ...

No wonder Mike watches from under the redwood:

    he knows too many of the names here!

How is it those who were never there are so cocksure!

Had Westmoreland not deceived the government ...

How rich my being

    to go to San Jose

    with my friend who was there!

Aboard the "Coast Starlight,"
California
November 25, 1984,
February 19, 1985

MY BROTHERS
WE SPENT OUR TIME
IN HELL YOU ARE
NOT FORGOTTEN BY
ME YOUR BROTHER WHO
LIVES, WE SHARED
A CIGAR OR TWO
I LEAVE THIS AS A
FINAL SMOKE FOR THE
BROTHERS I LOST
J.R. (CIGAR)
MAN

Vietnam
Veterans Brotherhood
"The Family" Inc.
"Together then Together again."
Welcome Home

_____

(   ) _____

KHE SANH

I left my heart to the sappers round Khe Sahn
And my soul was sold with my cigarettes to the black market man
I've had the Vietnam cold turkey
From the ocean to the Silver City
And it's only other Vets could understand

About the long forgotten darkside guarantees
How there were no V-day heroes in 1973
How we sailed into Sydney Harbour
Saw an old friend but couldn't kiss her
She was lined and I was home to the lucky land

And she was like so many more from that time on
Their lives were all so empty, till they found their chosen one
And their legs were often open
But their minds were always closed
And their hearts were held in fast suburban chains
And the legal pads were yellow, hours long, paypacket lean
And the telex writers clattered where the gunships once had been
But the carparks made me jumpy
And I never stopped the dreams
Or the growing need for speed and novacaine

So I worked across the country from end to end
Tried to find a place to settle down, where my mixed up life could mend
Held a job on an oil rig
Flying choppers when I could
But the nightlife nearly drove me round the bend

And I've travelled round the world from year to year
And each one found me aimless, one more year the more for wear
And I've been back to South East Asia
And the answer sure ain't there
But I'm drifting North, to check things out again

You know the last plane out of Sydney's almost gone
Only seven flying hours, and I'll be landing in Hong Kong
There ain't nothing like the kisses
From a jaded Chinese princess
I'm gonna hit some Hong Kong matress all night long

Well the last plane out of Sydney's almost gone
Yeah the last plane out of Sydney's almost gone
And it's really got me worried
I'm going nowhere and I'm in a hurry
And the last plane out of Sydney's almost gone.   COLD CHISEL, 1978

    You shall not grow old,
    As we here, who are left grow old.
    Age shall not weary you, nor the years condemn,
    At the going down of the sun, and in the morning,
    We WILL remember you.

    Death cannot rob you of your gallant deeds,
    For greater love hath no man
    Than he maketh the ultimate sacrifice
    And layeth his life down for his brother.

    You are gone, but will never be forgotten.

    LEST WE FORGET

Love from Australia.

Let all men know that this is holy ground.
Neither decay nor time shall ruin this sacred place,
For it is built, not only in granite,
But also in the hearts of men.
It shall stand here forever.
Therefore, instead of pity, praise.
The sacrifice of a nation lies here.

with love from Australia.

AUSTRALIA 45c

POSTCODE

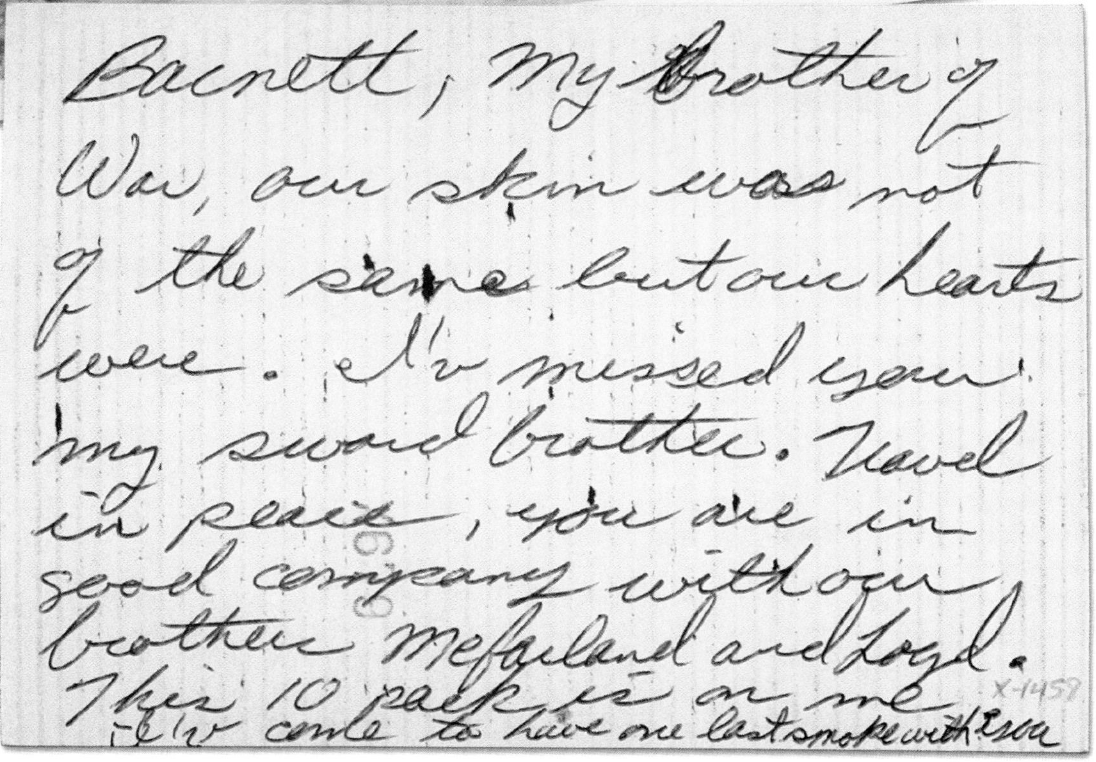

Barnett, My Brother of
War, our skin was not
of the same but our hearts
were. I'v missed you
my sword brother. Navel
in peace, you are in
good company with our
brother McFarland and Loyd.
This 10 pack is on me
I'v come to have one last smoke with you

X-1458

McFarland,
To watch you die has been
the most painful encounter
of my life. I prayed for before
my laughter g Way. When I
turned my head in helplessness
your breath g live had stopped
I could no longer hear your
breathing then I knew that
you were at peace. Bless you
for you are the hero.

WMC 1997

Sharon,

Well at last I have a chance to answer a few letters. We're taking off few days rest right now. Mostly because we don't have enough men to do anything else. We ran into charlie too, our company & another all day. We only had [?]. They killed isn't bad. Quite a few wounded. I'm in a line company, they changed my original MOS. I was machine gunner, but since we have lost our fire team leader, I'm the new one for our team.

I made spfc last month if all goes well the next three months I might(?) get sgt.

When we first got here 12-15-67 we were at Cu Chi about 15 miles west of Saigon.

For Viet Nam. New Year we were at Ban Hoa, then we moved to Quang tri. Stayed there a month. New were at Hue. Don't know how long we'll stay around here.

The weather changes when you go half down south, + cold up north. We weren't to far from the DMZ when we were at Quang tri.

Well Sharon, this is it for now your cup our [?] dinner call & [?] but let's go to T.T. Spend a few days with you, Grandmother.

Hoping that you & Manuela are in the best of health.

Sincerely,
Bill

---

3 Southlanders Killed In Viet

Three southland servicemen were among 12 California men reported by the Defense Department Friday as killed in action in Vietnam.

Army dead were Spec. 4 William Vazquez, son of Mrs. Gloria Van Gorder, 4642 Suite Drive, Huntington Beach, and PFC. Joseph C. Carvajal, husband of Mrs. Donna D. Carvajal, 10750 Tonibar St., Norwalk.

Marine Corps dead was PFC. Richard D. Hall, son of Mrs. Ruth H. Hall, 7348 S. Newlin Ave., Whittier.

IF YOU KNOW THIS MAN,
PLEASE WRITE OR CALL
COLLECT:

RONALD E. McCOOL
449 MARTIN ROAD

* (PAX MENTIS) *

THANK YOU VERY MUCH!

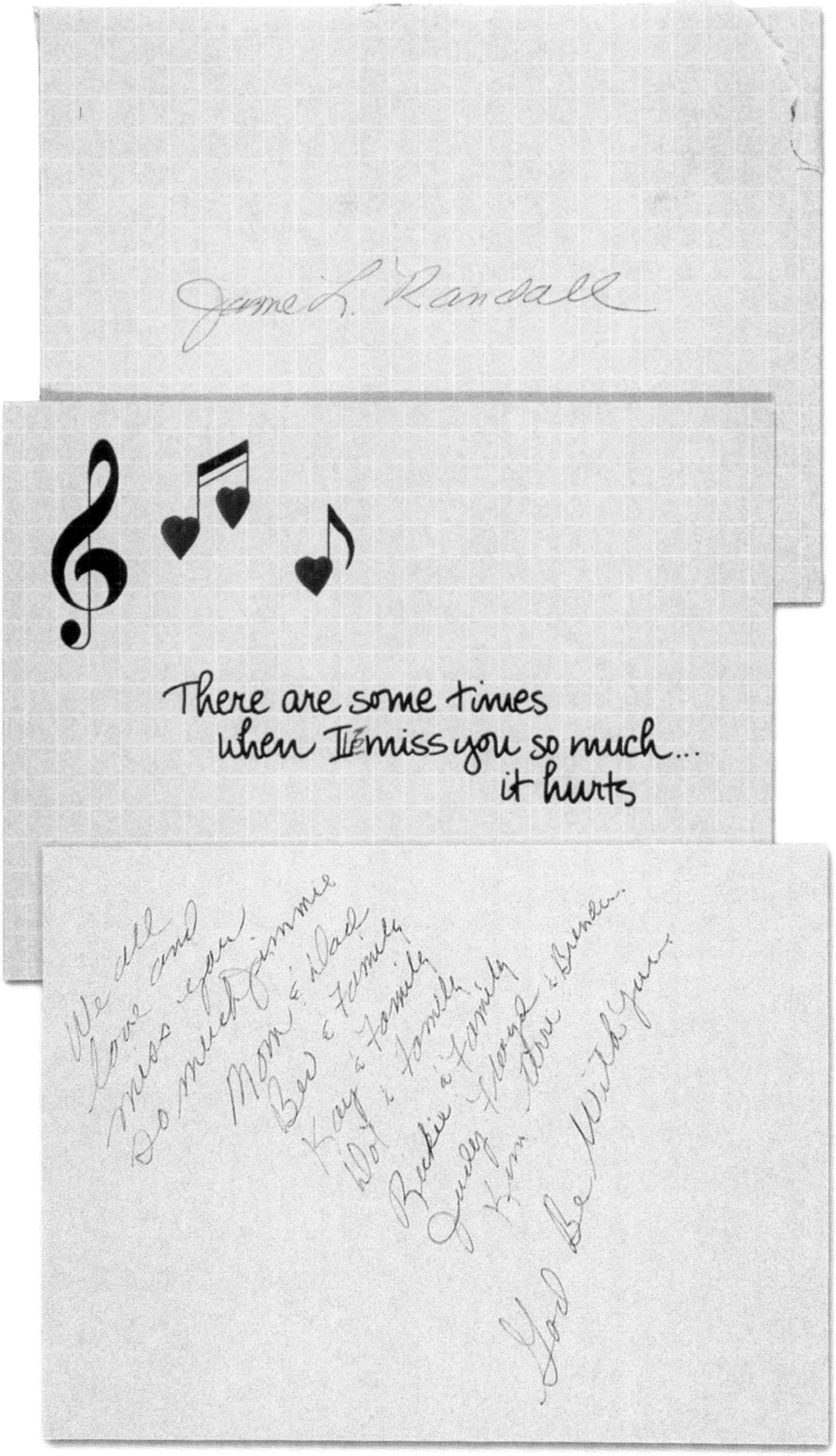

There are some times
when I miss you so much...
it hurts

We all
love and
miss you
so much Jimmie
Mom & Dad
Bro & Family
Kay & Family
Dot & Family
Buckie & Family
Sunday, George & Brenda
& am there love you
God Be With You

LTJG DAVID BROSTROM

IS HEREBY POSTHUMOUSLY AWARDED LIFE MEMBERSHIP
INTO THE COAST GUARD COMBAT VETERANS ASSOCIATION
IN HONOR OF THE SACRIFICE HE GAVE WHILE SERVING
HIS COUNTRY IN THE UNITED STATES COAST GUARD
THIS THE 11TH DAY OF NOVEMBER 1992

1959

IN HONOR OF THE MEN AND WOMEN OF
THE ARMED FORCES OF THE UNITED
STATES WHO SERVED IN THE VIETNAM
WAR, THE NAMES OF THOSE WHO GAVE
THEIR LIVES AND OF THOSE WHO REMAIN
MISSING ARE INSCRIBED IN THE ORDER
THEY WERE TAKEN FROM US

DAVID C BROSTROM

OUR NATION HONORS THE COURAGE
SACRIFICE AND DEVOTION TO DUTY AND
COUNTRY OF ITS VIETNAM VETERANS.
THIS MEMORIAL WAS BUILT WITH
PRIVATE CONTRIBUTIONS FROM
THE AMERICAN PEOPLE.
NOVEMBER 11, 1982

1975

CWOII James Mitchell and
SP/5 James J. Onetz Jr. taken
at Bien Hoa Air Base in
April 1968

Mr. Mitchell was killed
in action in June or July of 1968
Rep. of S Vietnam   23 July 68
Call Sign for AC 185 & Mr Mitchell
was Dragon 38.

1965 - 1985
E.F.A.
20th REUNION
July 4, 19
Dear Pip,
I'm bringing you this
cup from our class
reunion. You were there
with me even if no
one else saw you. It has
taken me a long time
to come to terms with
coming home.
would have
man. You
nice boy.
be that
my heart.
leave you
knowing
with God.
leaving the
for Dixon
You were
was the
job. He got
that damn war—
but he did turn out to be
your kind of guy.
You won after all—
Here I am this forty

2 E Line 131

Milton L. Olive III
PFC, U.S.A.
1946-1965

They named a college
in Chicago for you, Man.

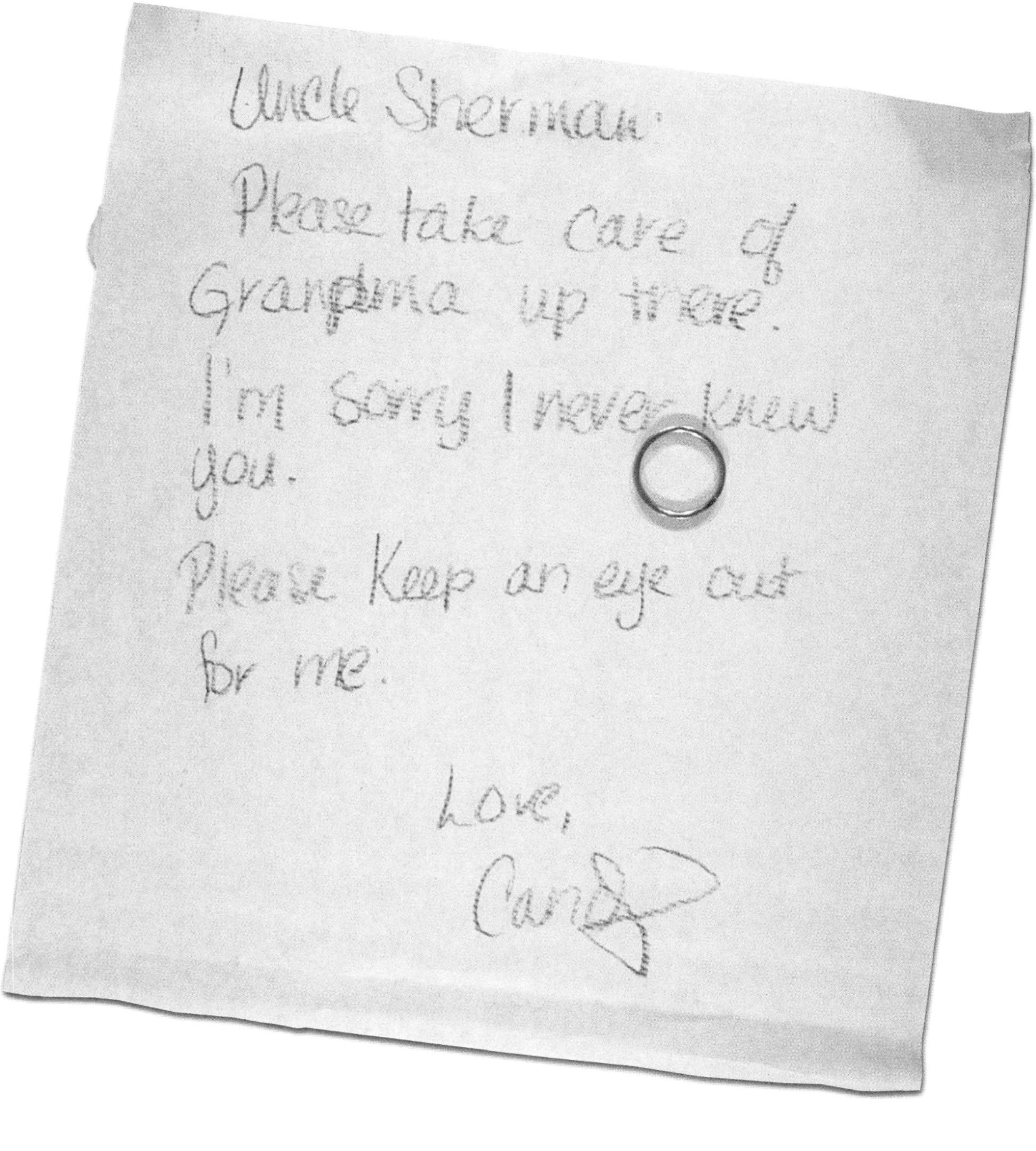

Uncle Sherman:

Please take care of Grandma up there.

I'm sorry I never knew you.

Please Keep an eye out for me.

Love,

Candy

Dedication

MICHAEL JOSEPH GALBRAITH

The members of the Class of 1967 dedicate this yearbook to
the memory of Michael Joseph Galbraith, who as a graduate of
R.C.S., was the first member of this community to give his life while
serving his country in the Vietnam conflict.

We dedicate this yearbook to a boy we all know, who died as a
man we will all remember.

ROSCOE CENTRAL SCHOOL
ROSCOE   N.Y. 12776

BOARD OF EDUCATION
PETER B. JOHNSTON, PRESIDENT
LORRAINE M. MIESNER, VICE PRESIDENT
DANIEL A. BALDO
THERESA M. BULL
W. KIMBALL SPRAGUE

BARRY L. SCHOENHOLZ, PH. D.
SUPERINTENDENT
MICHAEL J. WILLIAMS, PH. D.
ASSISTANT SUPERINTENDENT

607-498-4126

March 24, 1985

   We the graduating class of 1985 have traveled to our Nation's capitol
and wish to leave this flag in dedication to a former graduate of our school.
This flag has been carried from its place next to the monument in memoriam of
Michael J. Galbraith, located on our athletic field, in Roscoe, New York.

   Though none of us knew Michael, through our years of study we have come
to an understanding of why he and more than 55,000 other Americans so val-
iantly gave their lives for their country in Vietnam.

   We leave this presentation behind as our own monument, that the 32 members
of this graduating class of 1985, Roscoe Central School, Roscoe, New York have
not forgotten.

Barry L. Schoenholz
Superintendent

Raymond Pomeroy
Class President

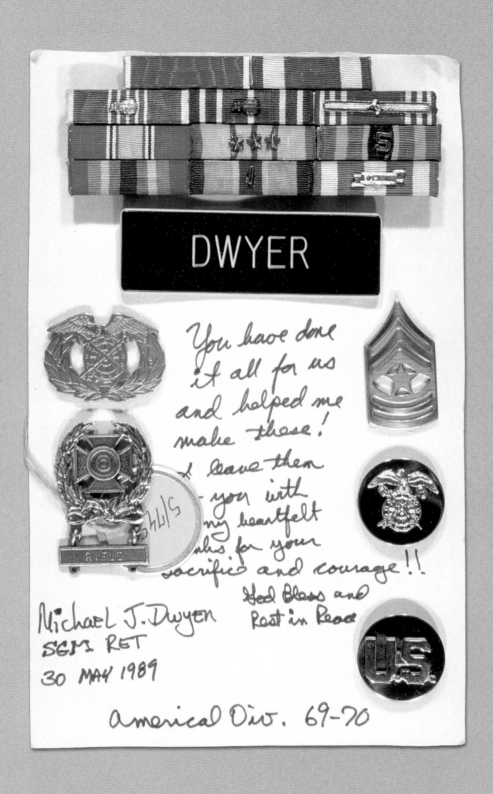

DWYER

You have done it all for us and helped me make these! I leave them to you with my heartfelt thanks for your sacrifice and courage!!

God Bless and Rest in Peace

Michael J. Dwyer
SGM RET
30 MAY 1989

America Div. 69-70

Pfc. Barry Berger killed in Vietnam

Barry H. Berger

Funeral services were held Tuesday for Pfc. Barry Howard Berger, 21, of Ocean City, who was killed in action Jan. 10 during combat operations near Chu Lai, South Vietnam.

Berger was the son of Mr. and Mrs. Albert Berger of Ocean City. He was in the Americal Division of the 75th Infantry (Rangers) of Army.

Berger was a 1967 graduate of Stephen Decatur High School and had attended American University in Washington, D.C.

In addition to his parents, he is survived by a brother, Harvey L. Berger, a student at the University of Maryland, and his paternal grandmother, Mrs. Tilly Berger.

Berger had been in Vietnam only a short time. He graduated from the 23rd Infantry Division Ranger Recondo School Dec. 4 as the Honor and Distinguished graduate.

In a letter of commendation from his infantry captain, Berger was cited as demonstrating outstanding mental and physical qualities in his ability to learn quickly and perform in a combat environment.

Berger was assigned to an operation team which is helicoptered to a surveillance area for reconnaisance and later picked up.

Funeral services were held in the Holloway Funeral Home in Salisbury. Interment was in the United Hebrew Cemetary in Baltimore.

The family suggests that, as a tribute to the memory of the deceased, contributions may be made to the Barry Berger Memorial Fund, in care of Beth Israel Congregation Salisbury.

In Honor of
Michael Wheeler
"Native American"
X - P.O.W.
1967 - 1969

America's Forgotten Minority

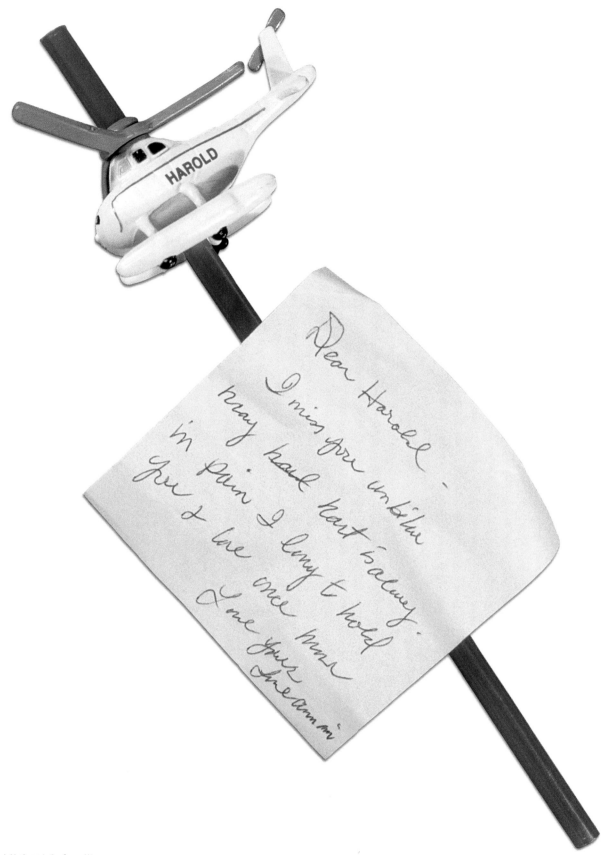

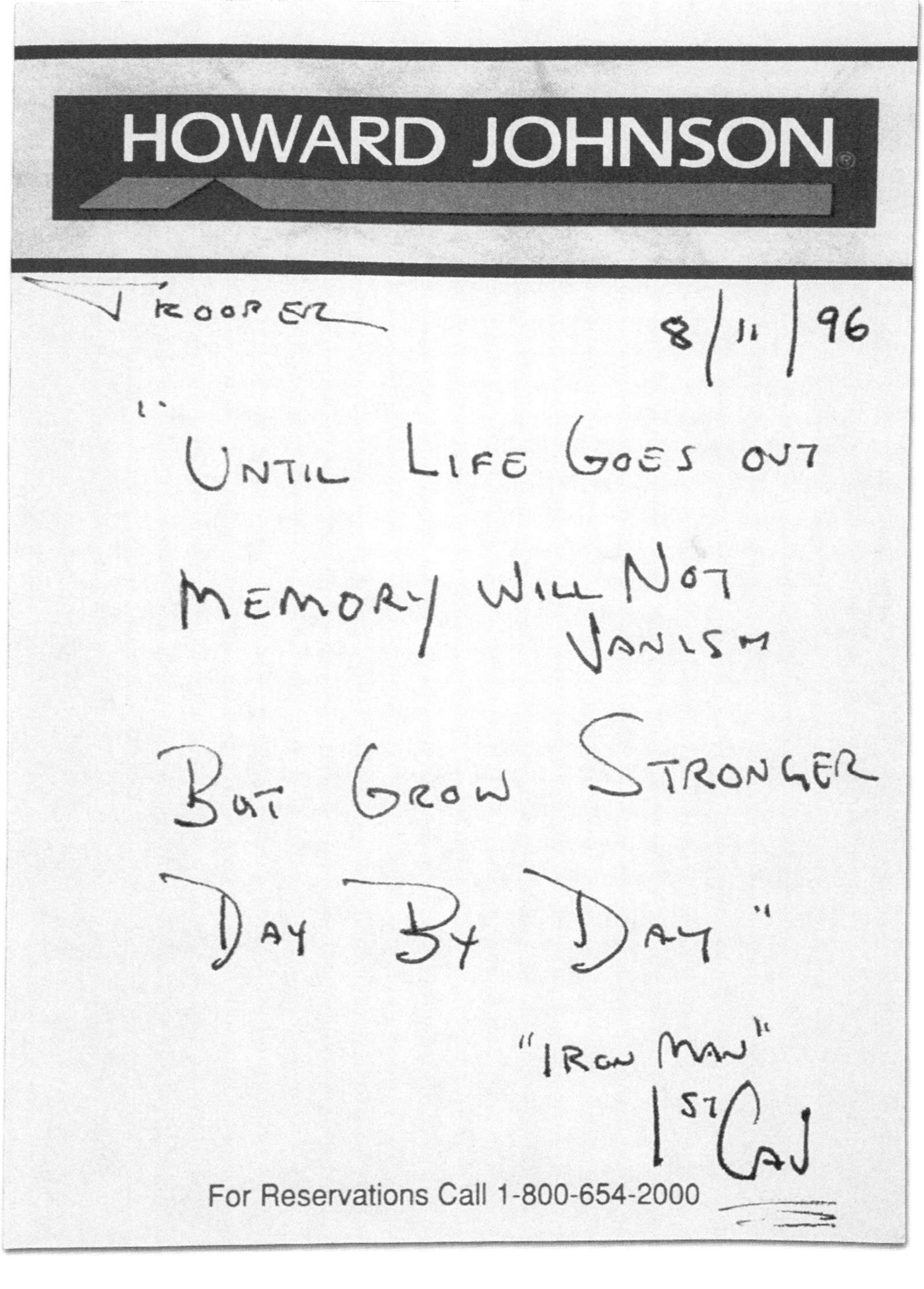

HOWARD JOHNSON

TROOPER   8/11/96

"UNTIL LIFE GOES OUT

MEMORY WILL NOT
                    VANISH

BUT GROW STRONGER

DAY BY DAY"

                    "IRON MAN"
                    1ST CAV

For Reservations Call 1-800-654-2000

"AND THE LION ROARS"

IT IS THE LION
THAT SCREAMS IN YOUR SOUL
IT IS THAT WHICH YOU TALK OF
YOU CAN NOT SPEAK OF.

NOT OF THIS WORLD
THE 'NAM LIVES INSIDE
YOU GOT OUT
BUT DID YOU SURVIVE?

YOU ARE MY VIET NAM
DANGEROUS AND EXCITING
EMOTIONAL AND TRAUMATIC...

HOLLOW IS THE HEART
THAT CAN NO LONGER HEAR
ITS OWN TEARS
BLOODS SPURTS FROM YOUR MIND
THE BODIES OF YOUR BROTHEREN
AWAKEN
IN THE NIGHT
ECHOES AND CRIES
        "THERE ARE TOO MANY!"
          "NO, NO DON'T!"
              "LOOK OUT!"
          "FUCK!"
WORDS MUMBLED
AS YOU SLEEP
LOVER, I KNOW
I CAN NOT GO
WHERE YOU HAVE GONE
HEART HARDENED
CONSTANT REMINDERS
DON'T CRY-DON'T CRY
NO LONGER CRIES
BUT WEEPS SILENTLY ALONE.

EMOTIONS
IN A BODY BAG
LIE
PAIN
UNRECOGNIZED
AND THE LION ROARS
SCREAMING NOW
IN MY SOUL...
                    Stacey Goodman '94

FOR R.F.
I WILL LOVE
YOU FOREVER...

To: Martin Powers

Water & sand from
Lake Winnipesaukee
New Hampshire.

FROM: In old summer
vacation freind at
Bright Horizon Cottage

Love, Theresa-Marie Figueiredo Pimental
Dartmouth, Mass.

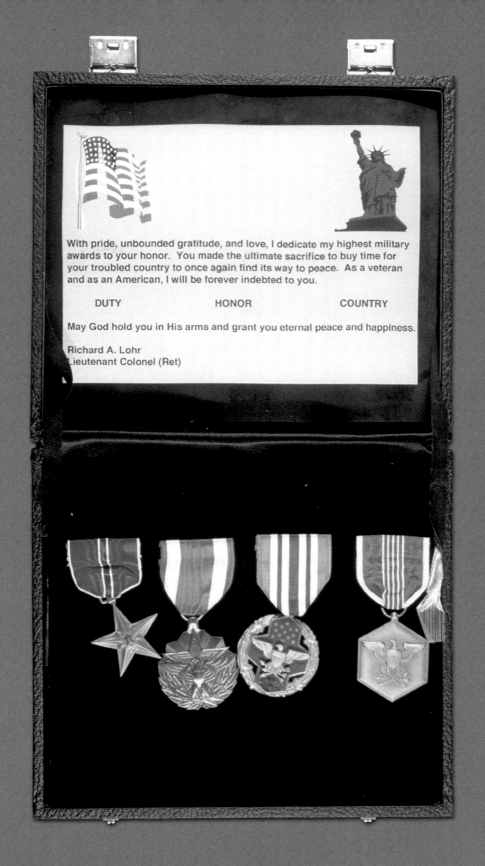

With pride, unbounded gratitude, and love, I dedicate my highest military awards to your honor. You made the ultimate sacrifice to buy time for your troubled country to once again find its way to peace. As a veteran and as an American, I will be forever indebted to you.

DUTY   HONOR   COUNTRY

May God hold you in His arms and grant you eternal peace and happiness.

Richard A. Lohr
Lieutenant Colonel (Ret)

DEPARTMENT OF THE ARMY
18th Aviation Company (Air Mbl FW)
APO San Francisco 96238

4 SEP 1967

Mrs. Delores Jones

New York

Dear Mrs Jones:

It is with genuine heartfelt sympathy that I undertake the writing of this letter. You undoubtedly have been notified that your husband, Chief Warrant Officer Wayne E. Jones, is missing. I will attempt to relate to you all of the information available surrounding Wayne's disappearance.

Wayne departed on the daily courier flight at 10:00 AM on 17 August. His schedule required him to make several stops along the route and return to his home station at Pleiku by 5 PM. After takeoff from his last stop at 4:25 PM, he made a radio transmission at 4:30 PM. Wayne failed to land at Pleiku within his estimated time of arrival. Within a short time, a search of all of the friendly airfields within his range of flight had been accomplished. However, due to increasing darkness and deteriorating weather conditions, a visual search by air could not begin until morning. Early the next morning all aircraft available in the area began an extensive search, flying hundreds of hours, covering the dense jungle and mountainous terrain over which Wayne would have flown. As of this date the airplane and it's crew have not been found. However, we are continuing to cover the area in great detail daily.

Wayne was one of the most respected and well liked officers in this unit. He had made many friends all of whom recognized him to be an outstanding pilot and a fine officer. All of us share your anxiety in anticipation of finding him.

If I can be of any assistance to you, please feel free to call upon me. I will consider it an honor to help.

Sincerely yours,

James T. Bri

JAMES T. BRIDGES
Maj, IN
Commanding

1959

HERMAN F RUBIN

1975

OUR NATION HONORS THE COURAGE
SACRIFICE AND DEVOTION TO DUTY AND
COUNTRY OF ITS VIETNAM VETERANS
THIS MEMORIAL WAS BUILT WITH
PRIVATE CONTRIBUTIONS FROM
THE AMERICAN PEOPLE.
NOVEMBER 11, 1982

SGT JAMES WALTER BISHOP
15W 49

ADIOS AMIGO

SGT. KELLY

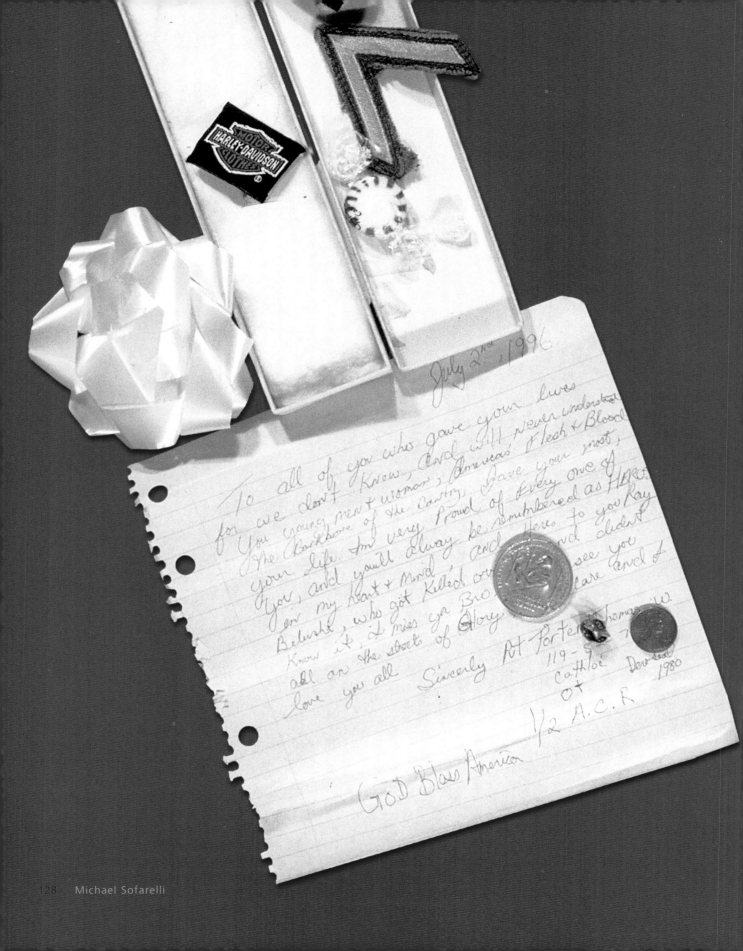

"DOC" AL PIERCE   KIA
HM2   24 FEB 66
                         CHU LAI VIETNAM

ATTACHED TO
BRAVO 1ST BN 12TH MARINES

KILLED BY .51 CAL VC MACHINE GUN

A daughter sees the distant battle,
    fire flashing o'er the field;

shattered men lie still and silent,
    never more a breath to yield;

Piercing deep into the vision,
    a father's face begins to form;

A daughter joins the distant battle,
    fighting to keep his memory warm.

Poem dedicated to Becky Womack — Daughter
Written by Robert Weeks — Nephew

In loving memory of
ROBERT LEE WOMACK
U.S. Marine Corps

January, 1930 — October, 1965

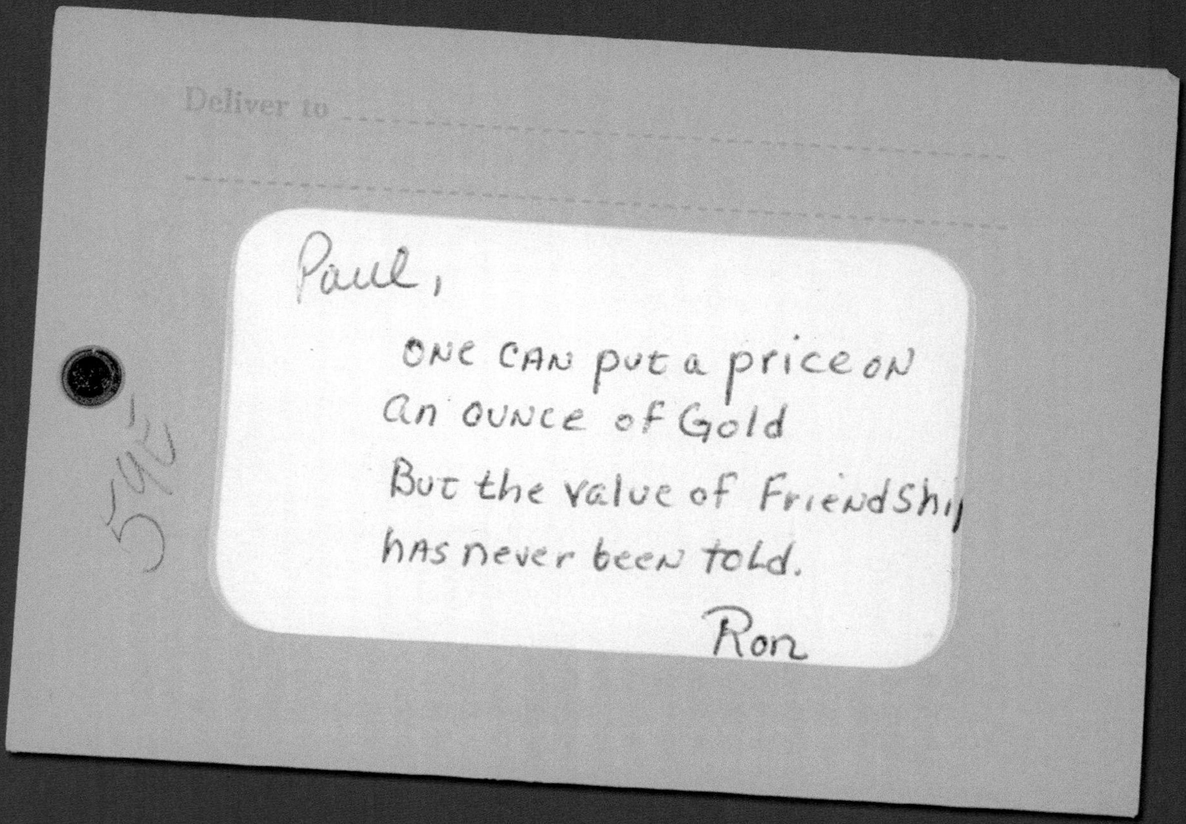

Deliver to

Paul,

one can put a price on
an ounce of Gold
But the value of Friendship
has never been told.

Ron

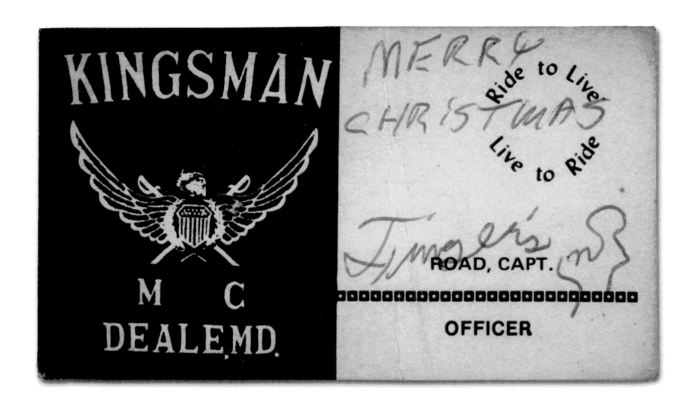

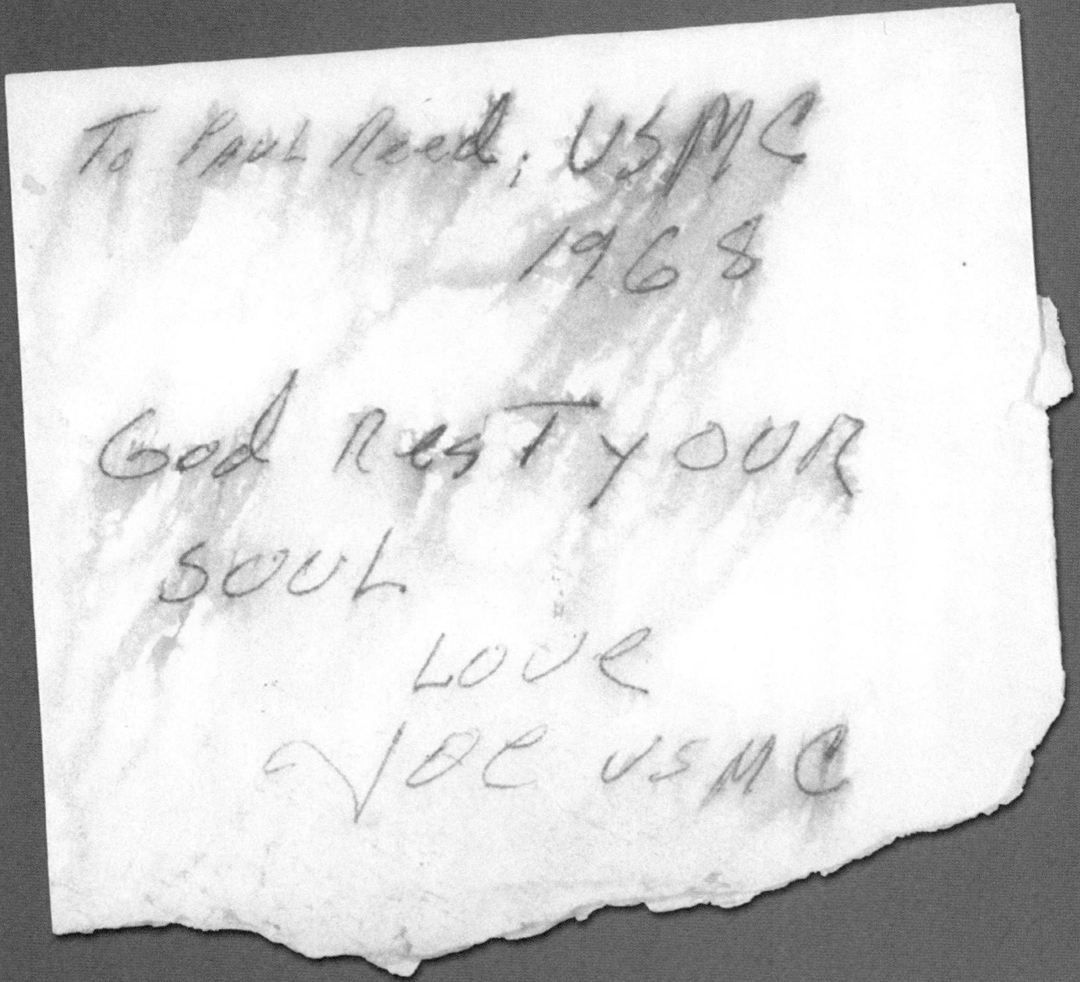

To Paul Reed; USMC
1968

God Rest Your
Soul
Love
Joe USMC

20 Feb. 70.

Dear Mike,

It's nice to Meet you. This picture was taken on My Graduation Day April 69. Good luck & God Bless you.

Love, (sis),
(Lopz   Elizabeth

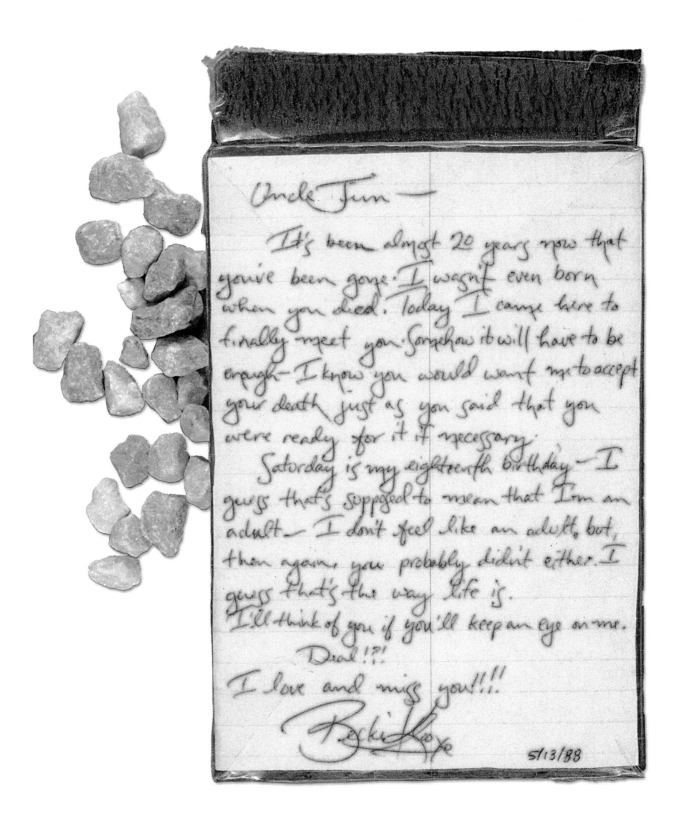

Uncle Jim—

It's been almost 20 years now that you've been gone. I wasn't even born when you died. Today I came here to finally meet you. Somehow it will have to be enough—I know you would want me to accept your death just as you said that you were ready for it if necessary.

Saturday is my eighteenth birthday—I guess that's supposed to mean that I'm an adult—I don't feel like an adult, but, then again, you probably didn't either. I guess that's the way life is.

I'll think of you if you'll keep an eye on me. Deal!?!

I love and miss you!!!!

Becki xoxo

5/13/88

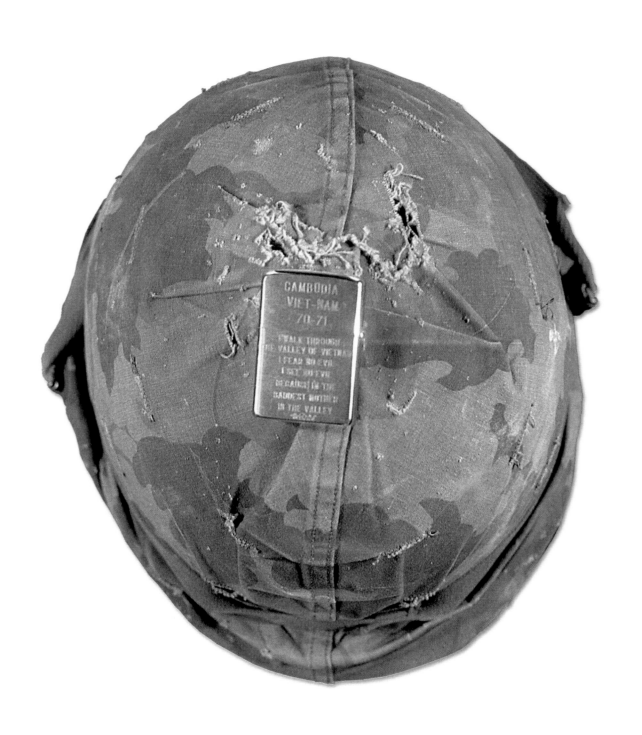

Paul and I "showing off" the "Eagle, Globe & Anchor"

02 Oct. 1965

ATT.

59E

Aug. 13, 1985
To my dear nephew
Ralphie. God
bless you. We
Are all praying
for you. we miss
you & love
you.
Auntie Cindy

CHARles Terrel
SP4 ~~AR MC~~ AR
29 Aug 42
13 Feb 66   FAiRMON NC.
THUrmont MArylAnd
┌─────────┐
│ PAnel   │   Line
│ ~~16~~ 0   │   29
└─────────┘
5E

JAck   PFC Airy
17 MAR 46
25 July 66 OH.
BeAllsvilA

9E 76

I love you and miss
you very much.

This hat is from CPT.
MOSES A. WEST US Army
for
FRED JENKINS, MY UNCLE

IN HONOR AND MEMORY OF MY
FRIEND'S.

JIM GRAHAM - CAPT. USMC
JAN WILSON - CPL   USMC
DELBERT LEASURE - L/CPL USMC
KEN BUGGNER - PFC   USMC
JERRY STENBERG - L/CPL USMC
KENNETH ALLAN - PFC   USMC
BILL DALTON - PFC   USMC
                    SEMPER FIDELIS
                    YOUR FRIEND
                    JACKIE SCHWANE

C-1-13   26th MARINES KHE SANH

NAVA--NATIVE AMERICAN AND VETERANS ALLIANCE IS A
NEW ORGANIZATION ESTABLISHED FOR NATIVE AMERICANS
AND MILITARY VETERANS.
WE WOULD LIKE FOR ALL NATIVE AMERICANS, VETERANS,
AND THEIR FAMILIES TO JOIN TOGETHER FOR THE PURPOSES
LISTED ON THE OPPOSITE PAGE.

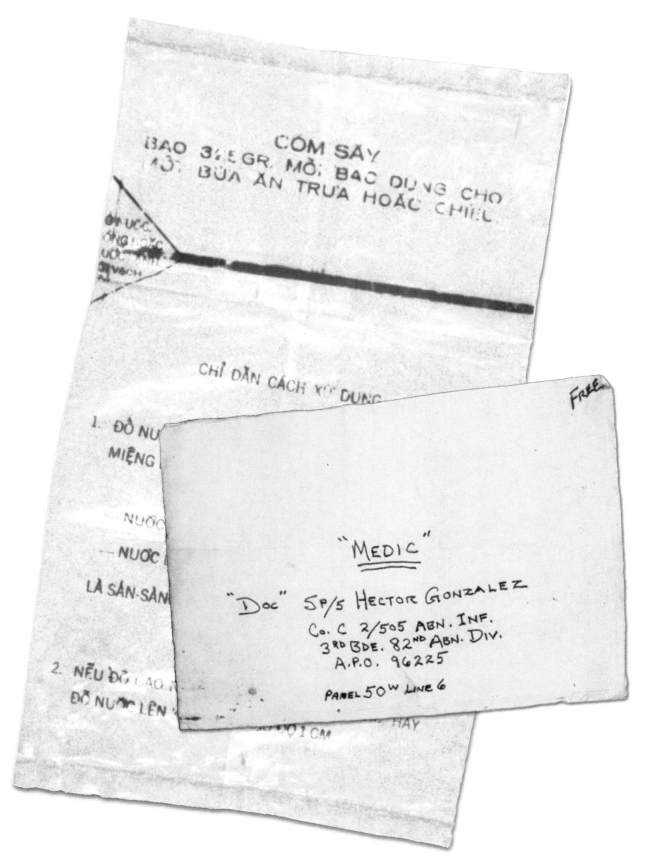

The Cross In My Pocket

I carry a cross in my pocket
A simple reminder to me
Of the fact that I am a Christian
No matter where I may be.

This little cross is not magic
Nor is it a good luck charm
It isn't meant to protect me
From every physical harm.

It's not for identification
For all the world to see
It's simply an understanding
Between my Savior and me.

When I put my hand in my pocket
To bring out a coin or key
The cross is there to remind me
Of the price He paid for me.

It reminds me, too, to be thankful
For my blessings day by day
And to strive to serve Him better
In all that I do and say.

It's also a daily reminder
Of the peace and comfort I share
With all who know my Master
And give themselves to His care.

So, I carry a cross in my pocket
Reminding no one but me
That Jesus Christ is Lord of my life
If only I'll let Him be.

Made in U.S.A.

We laughed, We lived
We loved We fought
and some of us died
I miss you
Mike Powell
USMC

Nam
65–66

To: Diane Evans and all the Nurses who served in Vietnam.

It was with great interest and satisfaction that I read about the $10,000.00 donation made by Chevron towards your cause.

I am a Vietnam veteran and I stand behind your effort. I am a member of Vietnam Veterans Of America Western Reserve Chapter # 439 in Chesterland, Ohio, and we discussed your cause at our meeting of March 23,1989. The unanimous decision of our organization was that we support your cause.

I currently am the committee chairman for our educational program. In this program we go into the local high schools and tell not only about the Vietnam War, but also how we feel about what we did. I did two tours of duty in Vietnam as a non commissioned officer in the United States Navy. One tour on a Destroyer Escort off the coast of Vietnam, and one tour on a U.S. Navy Swift Boat (PCF) making raids in the rivers and canals of the Ca Mau peninsula. My unit took a casualty rate of 82% during the time I was there. I did my share of killing and I saw my share of dying but I want you to know that before I ever heard of your cause I was giving a talk to high school students at South High School in Willoughby Ohio and after I told them my story, as bad as it was, I asked them a question. I asked the students what they thought was the toughest job in Vietnam. Not one of them had the same answer I did. I told them I thought it was being a nurse. I saw many of my brothers that were hit with a bullet or shrapnel or worse. Fortunately for me I only had to bear their misery for a short time until I could get them to a medivac chopper. You, on the other hand, had to live with that every minute you were there. I carry some awful memories in my mind of the horror and reality of war but I am sure I would not trade mine for yours. My job was to kill and unfortunately due to the mentality of the time I became very good at it. I am not proud of that, but I can't change it now. Your job was to heal and there is no doubt in my mind now which is a more honorable profession.

I have traveled this country extensively. I have been in big cities and small ones. I have been to our nations capital. I see statues and monuments all over this country of our military leaders. I have seen a monument that reaches hundreds of feet into the sky to honor a General. I have seen a monument of our soldiers raising a flag in some far away land. I have seen large monuments and I have seen small monuments. I have even seen monuments with a man sitting on a horse with a sword in his hand. I can drive in my own local communities and see tanks, and if I drive a little farther I can see fighter planes and guns and swords. I can go to museums and see bullets and rockets and handgrenades.

I can drive a little further to Buffalo New York and see the
U.S. Navy Park where they have made a permanent monument of a
destroyer, a gunboat and a submarine. I can see all these
heroes of our country whose job it was to kill other human
beings. I can see all these wonderful machines we have invented
for the sole purpose of destroying life. But if my son were to
ask me, Dad, where can we go to see a monument to the women of
this country who saved lives, I would sadly have to say, I am
sorry son, I don't know. I think that says something very sad
about this world.

You deserve your statue more than I can ever put into
words. If it wasn't for you I would not have the pleasure of
many of my friends company because their names would have been
on The Wall. If it wasn't for you The Wall would have to be
much bigger than it is now because all of my brothers you saved
would have to have their names on The Wall also.

You will have your statue, but I only wish the world
would put me in charge of it, because you would not have to pay
for it. I would make the leaders of this world who send their
children to other far off lands to die on the battlefields pay
for it. They talk of liberty and honor and justice while they
sit home and watch the earth run red with the blood of its sons
and daughters. I would make them come into your field hospitals
and see if any of their sons with parts of their arms or legs or
faces left behind in a rice paddy talk about honor or justice or
liberty or any of the other words that ring hollow while they
scream for their mothers and slowly and painfully their life
slips away from them. I would make them trade their arms for a
Purple Heart or their innocence for a Silver Star. I would make
them fill the body bags with what was left of their sons. If
they put me in charge of your statue she would not be next to
ours at The Wall. She would stand right where the "V" in The
Wall meets on top of the hill, and she would be one hundred feet
tall with her arms stretched out to each end of The Wall and a
tear in her eye to represent the sorrow you must feel for not
being able to save the lives of all the men and women whose
names are chiseled on it.

The day your statue is dedicated I will be there just
to give you a hug and say "THANK YOU".

Thank you, Joe,
with great
respect from all
the women who the me
served to all the me
served. We
love you. Love Carson Evans
NOV 10, 1987

Sincerely

Joe Muharsky

Joe Muharsky
PO2 U.S. NAVY
Black Berets
1966-1969

WE
REMEMBER
AUTREY MIDD.
SCH.
KENNESAW, GA.

15 Oct. 59   B-52/KC135 mid-air
collision occuring near the hamlet of
Glen Jean 75 miles SW of Louisville, Ky
B-52 wreakage from an
In memory of the B-52/KC135 crew members
who went down with their planes, especially
my father, Lt Harold E. Helmick KC135
Navigator. Given in memory by his son
Scott Helmick and family...

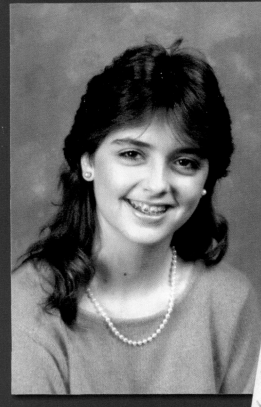

Dad, (Thomas Bump)
I feel more relieved
now that I've come.
I can believe it now
more than ever. I want
you to know that I
love you even though
I never knew you &
Mom still loves you
too. She always will
& Will &. Love always
Shawn M.
(1985)

Dear God,
Let in These [warriors]
They've [spent their]
Time in Hell.

For The 130 * Names
On This Wall From The
State of Wyoming,
I've Promised Your Moms & Dads, I will Not let
Them, We Get You. I've gotten very Close To many of
Them, We Love Them & Look out for Them, We can Never Take
Your Place

I knew you not,
I know you well
In my heart
and mind you dwell.

This blackened stone
stands tall and proud
And yet I stand alone
in the crowd.

The letters seem
to never end
To spell the names
of long lost men.

The cause for which
you were called to fight
It made no sense.
And cost your life.

And so I stand on hallowed ground
I leave a token small,
And never will I e'er forget
this place they call THE WALL.

Donna J. Adams
Palatka, Florida
Oct. 1992

IN MEMORY OF

WAYNE FULLAM, COL, USAF

THE USAF

RIVER RATS

18TH TFW

AND THE 67TH TFS

WILL REMEMBER

ONE HELL OF A PILOT

FOREVER!

NAME	DATE OF BIRTH	MILITARY SERVICE	RANK		DATE OF INCIDENT	CITY, MASS
ALLEN, Wayne Clouse	48 Mar 17	Army	E5	VS	70 Jan 10	Tewksbury
AVERY, Allen Jones	43 Feb 22	Air Force	E6	VS	72 Apr 06	Auburn
BAXTER, Bruce Raymond	31 Sep 28	Army	E8	LA	67 Nov 08	Lowell
BERESIK, Eugene Paul	33 Mar 03	Air Force	04	VN	68 May 31	Webster
BERUBE, Kenneth Allen	43 Oct 30	Marine Corps	02	VS	67 Aug 11	Monson
BIFOLCHI, Charles Lawrence	43 Oct 27	Air Force	02	VA	68 Jan 08	Quincy
BOLES, Warren William	40 Dec 14	Navy	02	VN	68 Jan 18	Marblehead Neck
BORONSKI, John Arthur	44 Jul 24	Army	E6	CB	70 Mar 24	Ware
BOTT, Russell Peter	36 Sep 05	Army	E6	LA	66 Dec 02	Worcester
COAKLEY, William Francis	38 Aug 12	Navy	04	VN	66 Sep 13	Lenox
COCHRANE, Deverton C.	48 Dec 15	Army	E6	CB	70 Jun 17	Brookline
COLLARMORE, Allan Philip Jr.	38 Dec 22	Navy	03	VN	67 Feb 04	Worcester
COOK, Joseph Francis	49 Jan 15	Marine Corps	E3	VS	68 May 10	Foxboro
CZERWONKA, Paul Steven	49 May 20	Marine Corps	E2	VS	68 May 10	Stoughton
DONATO, Paul Nicholas	40 Mar 14	Navy	E6	LA	68 Feb 17	Boston
DUNN, Joseph Patrick	42 Sep 17	Navy	02	CH	68 Feb 14	Hull
EARLE, John Stiles	41 Jul 03	Navy	03	VS	70 Jan 22	Westfield
ELLIOT, Robert M.	29 Nov 08	Air Force	03	VN	66 Feb 14	Springfield
PITTS, Richard A.	46 Feb 23	Army	E6	LA	68 Nov 30	Abington
GERALD, Joseph E.	48 Nov 25	Army	E3	VS	67 May 31	Northbridge
William D.	38 Nov 14	Navy	03	VN	66 Mar 01	Brockton
GA Frederick Thomas	36 Nov 16	Air Force	E5	LA	61 Mar 23	Plymouth
GAUGH ger Conrad	46 Jun 24	Marine Corps	E4	VS	67 May 01	Belchertown
GRAVES, d Campbell	44 Aug 05	Navy	01	VN	67 May 25	Sunderland
GREENLEAF, h G.	44 Oct 06	Navy	03	VS	72 Apr 14	W. Newton
HARPER, Rich	41 Oct	Army	W3	VS	65 May 19	Burlington
HAUER, Robert	46 29		02	VS	70 Sep 05	Brookline
HENN, John Robert	Feb 11		W2	VS	72 May 24	Sutton
HERRIN, Henry Howar		y	01	VN	68 Jan 01	W. Springfield
HOLMES, David Hugh	3 26	For	03	LA	66 Mar 15	Belmont
HOLT, Robert Alan	1	arine s	03	VN	68 Sep 19	Reading
KASTER, Leonard Lee	ep 24	ir	02	VS	64 Aug 06	Holyoke
KELLEY, Daniel Mar		Arm	E4	VS	68 Apr 25	Dorchester
KING, Paul Chest	Mar 17	Ar	E3	LA	68 May 04	Waltham
KINSMEN, Geral ncis	un 12	my	02	VS	71 Jan 15	Foxboro
KUSTIGIAN, M J.	49 Mar	Navy	E7	VN	68 May 05	Worcester
LEAVER, Job ray Jr.	33 Aug 17	Navy	05	VN	72 May 08	Arlington
LOHEED, H B.	24 Oct 15	Navy	05	VN	66 Feb 01	Middleboro
MACCANN, y Elmer	31 Dec 11	Air Force	04	VN	68 Mar 28	Marblehead
MAGNUSS James A. Jr.	34 Oct 14	Air Force	03	VN	65 Apr 04	Nahant
MCKEN Kenneth Dewey	45 Apr 03	Air Force	E3	LA	66 May 15	Auburn
MCLAU IN, Arthur V.	34 Mar 11	Air Force	E7	VN	72 Dec 20	Roxbury
MILLE Carleton Pierce Jr.	44 Jun 23	Navy	02	VN	71 Jan 06	Melrose
MORIN Richard G.	44 Jul 08	Marine Corps	02	LA	68 Dec 20	Tewksbury
MULLE illiam F.	35 Mar 28	Marine Corps	03	LA	66 Apr 29	Brockton
OVERLOCK hn F.	36 Apr 06	Air Force	04	VN	68 Aug 16	Springfield
PAINTER, John rt Jr.	45 Mar 15	Navy	03	VN	71 Jun 18	Vineyard Haven
ROGERS, Edward Fra	48 Sep 29	Marine Corps	E2	VS	68 Mar 12	Roslindale
SANSONE, James	24	Navy	E3	VN	72 Aug 10	Norwood
SMITH, William M.		Army	E3	VS	69 Mar 03	Middleboro
STEPHENSON, Howard D.	37 Oc	Force	04	LA	72 Mar 29	Bolton
SULLIVAN, Martin Joseph	33 Jan 28		04	VS	67 Feb 12	Lawrence
TODD, Robert Jacy	48 May 25	Mar	E1	VS	67 May 09	North Easton
TUCKER, Edwin Byron	35 Feb 01	Navy	04	VN	67 Apr 24	Baldwinville
WALKER, O'Brien J.	33 Sep 27	Army	03	VS	65 May 23	Boston
WATERMAN, Craig Houston	43 Oct 14	Marine Corps	02	VS	67 Jul 30	Rehoboth
WAX, David J.	41 Aug 01	Air Force	02	VS	65 Dec 20	Brookline
WEITZ, Monek	50 Dec 19	Marine Corps	E1	VS	69 May 25	Roxbury
WYRE, Blair C.	29 May 23	Air Force	04	VN	66 Aug 12	Auburndale

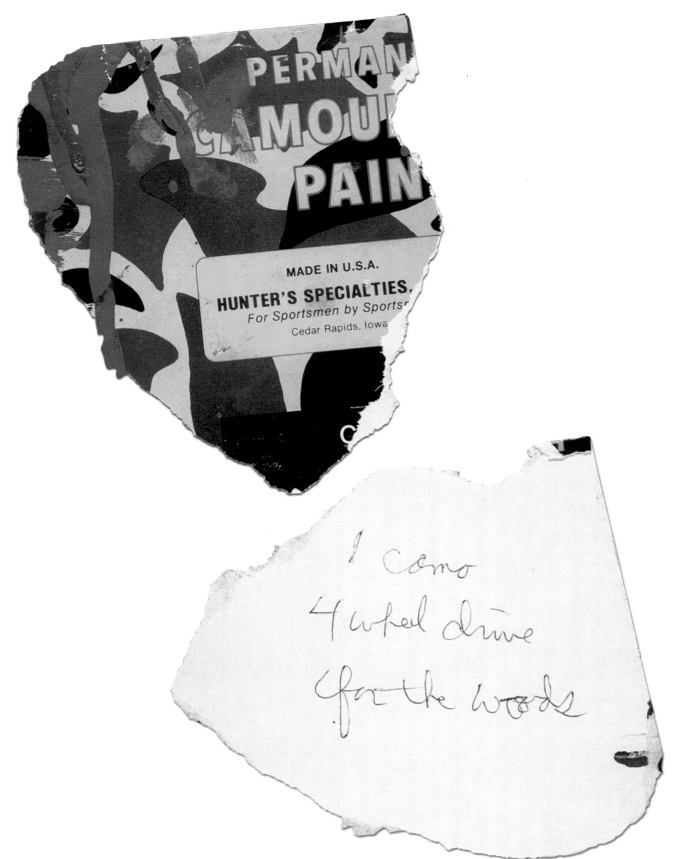

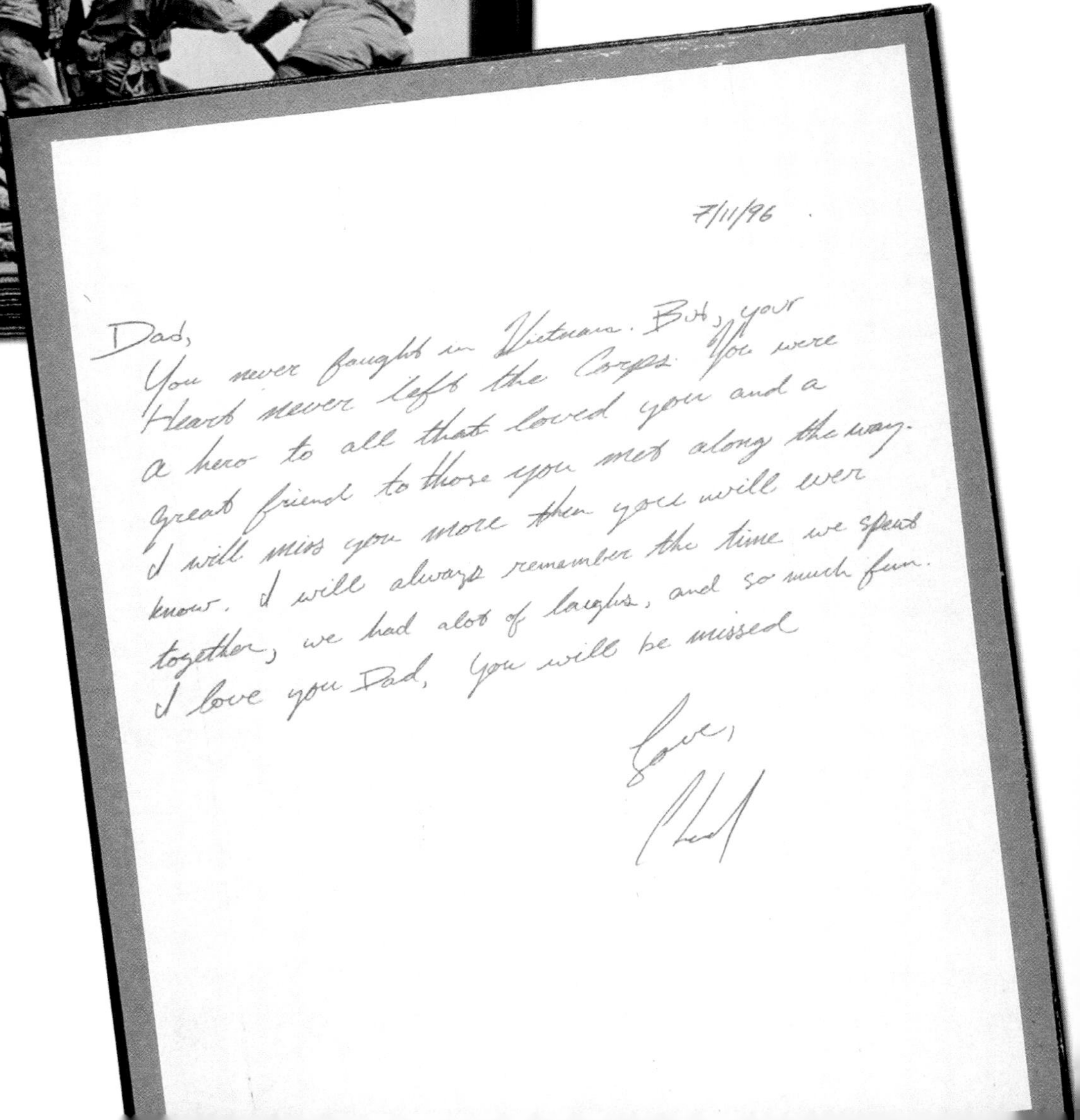

7/11/96

Dad,
You never fought in Vietnam. But, your Heart never left the Corps. You were a hero to all that loved you and a great friend to those you met along the way. I will miss you more then you will ever know. I will always remember the time we spent together, we had alot of laughs, and so much fun. I love you Dad, You will be missed

Love,
Phil

We did what we could but it was not enough because I found you here. All of you are not just names on this wall. you are alive. You're bloods on my hands, your screams in my ears, your eyes in my soul. I told you you'd be alright but I lied, please forgive me, I _ce your face in my sou_. I can't bear the thought. You told me about your wife, your kids your girl your mother. Then you died. I should have done more. Your pain is ours. Please go. I'll never forget your faces I can't, your shit shoe.

DEPARTMENT OF THE ARMY
HEADQUARTERS, FIFTH UNITED STATES ARMY
Fort Sam Houston, Texas 78234

SPECIAL ORDERS   17 November 1971
NUMBER   224
EXTRACT

2. TC 453. Following individual APPOINTED/DESIGNATED/CERTIFIED as
indicated.

BARNABA, ROBERT J.   CPT 1981 1st Av Co (WAHL-CO) Fort Riley,
Kansas 66442 FA

Authority: AR 95-1 VOCG 15 Nov 71
Designated as: NA
Certified as: NA
Appointed as: Instructor Pilot
Period: Indefinite
Purpose: To instruct in TH-13 Aircraft. USAAVNS trained in UH-1 and TH-13.
Effective date: 15 Nov 71
Special Instructions: Instructor Pilot is qualified to perform all phases of
                       flight instruction for the aircraft in which designated
                       and will be recognized in the specific series aircraft
                       when the requirements of paragraph 2-3b, AR 95-1, are
                       completed. Appropriate series notation will be entered
                       in Block 24, Remarks, of DA Form 759 (Part 1).

                                                    (ODCSO&T)

FOR THE COMMANDER:

                                    CHARLES W. RYDER, JR.
                                    Major General, GS
                                    Chief of Staff

FOSTER B. WATSON
Colonel, AGC
Adjutant General

DISTRIBUTION:
5 - CG, 1st Infantry Div and Fort Riley, KS 66442
5 - Indiv conc
5 - Avn Div, ODCSO&T
5 - AGAO (record set)

DEAR GLENN
        THANK YOU FOR YOUR
LION-HEARTEDNESS IN BONG SON
THIRTY YEARS AGO YOU MADE
YOUR WAY INTO MY HEART -- YOU
TAUGHT ME LESSONS ONLY ONE
WARRIOR CAN TEACH ANOTHER. I
HAVE COME TODAY TO SIMPLY
HONOR YOU, SIR.   BARRY OWEN
                        BROOKS

2/13/96

OMNI ✿ HOTELS®

MISS YOU OLD
BUDDY
DEAR BILL
(COWBOY)
BEEN A LONG
TIME BUT
I MADE IT...
TO BAD
GOOD MEM
GOTTA EAT
SO POLOTICKAL
CAN EAT
BETTER, YOUR
PAL ROCK MAN

1-800-THE-OMNI

66   67

To the 1's

You were always the
one when I was there and
are still No.#1
    Wines have changed
but my thoughts for yours
have never changed!
    There will come a time!
        Forever Another One
    Pointman — Sgt. James Baker 2/16 Inf.

Danny

It gets harder to remember what you look like. I have to keep looking in the high school yearbook.

We are having a 35th year class reunion in Aug. Imagine that 35 years ago in May we graduated with dreams and hopes and yours ended in Vietam. You are the only one from our class to die over there. I think we all wouldn't want that honor.

Butch Williams died this year from a heart attack and Donny Williams got killed by his old friend. She ran over him with a car. How ironic that was.

Its cold this Memorial day. I am trying to write without gloves and my fingers are freezing.

I will be back in the summer to visit this place that holds so many memories.

Your friend
Jimmy

P.S. I leave the bottle in memory of friendship

Will The Memories Remain ?

We were friends during high school and college. Sharing many a common event during those years.

Then you decided to follow your brothers tradition and join the Marines. We took the midnight train to Kansas City. Most of the time was spent trying to talk you out of joining and you trying to convince me that it was the right thing to do. I couldn't change your mind and the recruiter couldn't change mine, although he tried.

I was being clever and mailed to you a brochure I'd picked up at the Student Union about O.C.S. while you were in boot camp. You didn't tell me until after graduation that the brochure assured you a trip to the quonset with your D.I. Still you didn't complain.

Your orders read R.V.N. after you completed all your training . One patrol and weeks later they returned you to the world. Of course you never knew but I retraced our train trip. This time the signature was mine.

I still don't know why I made it back and you didn't. How lucky I've remained: With a wife, two daughters, and a son with James in his name.

It's been 18 years and you're not just a name carved in at 35E/9.

The memories still remain!
PFC James L. Siron

                                                    Bud

SOLDIER

I was that which others did not want to be.
I went where others feared to go. and did
what others Failed to do.
I asked nothing from those who gave nothing. and
reluctantly accepted the thought of eternal
loneliness··· should I fail.
I have seen the Face of terror;
Felt the stinging cold of Fear;
and enjoyed the sweet taste of a moments love.
I have cried, Pained, and Hoped······
but most of all,
I have lived times others would say were best
forgotten.
At least someday I will be
able to say that I was
proud of what I was··· a Soldier

As I was thinking
of you today ...

A smile tickled my face

all my love,
Joy

DAYS OF **REMEMBRANCE**

IN MEMORY DAY

In Memory Day is both a day and a program to honor all veterans who have died as a result of the Vietnam War but whose deaths do not fit the United States Department of Defense's criteria for inclusion upon the Vietnam Veterans Memorial in Washington, D.C. Only the names of those who died in combat are currently inscribed on the black granite walls. There are many veterans who die every year prematurely as a result of the war and whose names will never be commemorated in black granite.

Every year on the third Monday in April, family and friends of In Memory honorees gather at the Wall for the In Memory Day ceremony. During the ceremony, the names of all In Memory honorees are read aloud by family members or friends. At the conclusion of the ceremony, certificates bearing the honorees' names as well as other tributes are placed and left at the base of the Vietnam Veterans Memorial. These tributes are collected by the National Park Service and stored in its permanent collection. The honorees are then included in an In Memory honor roll book that serves as a reminder of their sacrifice and service to their country.

MOTHER'S DAY

Thousands of women lost their sons (and a few of their daughters) as a result of the Vietnam War. Mother's Day at the Vietnam Memorial is an important and emotional event for Vietnam veterans and their families. Each year since 1999, the Mother's Day at The Wall Ceremony has recognized the sacrifices of mothers as they honor and remember their lost sons who have given their lives for defense of their country. Every year the Vietnam Veterans Memorial Fund honors these American Gold Star Mothers for their sacrifice with a ceremonial Mother's Day card reading at the Vietnam War Memorial. Cards created by Washington, D.C., area students, teachers and other organization such as the Girl Scouts of America, are read aloud and then placed at the base of the Wall by a fallen soldier's mother.

MEMORIAL DAY

For more than 25 years, thousands of veterans and their families have descended upon the Vietnam Veterans Memorial in Washington, D.C., each year to honor and remember those men and women who have given their lives defending their country. The annual Memorial Day observance at the Wall is a time to pay tribute not just to veterans from Vietnam, but veterans from all wars. On this day, the Vietnam Veterans Memorial Fund (VVMF) and the United States National Park Service cohost ceremonies to honor Vietnam veterans and all servicemen and women of all U.S. wars.

Memorial Day ceremonies held at the Wall in years past have included individuals from all walks of life. Presidents Ronald Reagan, George H. W. Bush, and Bill Clinton have all addressed the record crowds at past ceremonies. Several U.S. senators, congressmen, and cabinet members have also been given the honor of speaking as well as Bob Hope and Ted Koppel. Performers have included the country music group Alabama, Pat Boone, and Irish tenor John McDermott.

In 2005, Memorial Day ceremonies included the official recognition of the names of four servicemen added to the Wall.

FATHER'S DAY

LTC Anthony V. Fasolo, USA (Ret)
Vietnam Veterans Memorial Volunteer

Each year for the past ten years Father's Day has meant to me "Roses at the Wall"

Each year we honor those whose names are on the Wall because they gave their all
I listen to the "Oldies but Goodies" station as I drive to DC on this unusually cool clear day
Tunes from the 60s and 70s help return me to my time in 'Nam when we were in the fray
Each year for the past ten years, Father's Day has meant to me "Roses at the Wall"

At the Wall I now meet with friends, old and new, and we ask each other "How Are You?"
"When were you in Nam?" "82d Airborne?", "Cu Chi, 25th Division?"
"And how about You?" "Were you there too?", "Phu Bai", "Quang Tri",
"Is that where you hurt your knee?"
"There are still six not accounted for but last week we buried O'Brien and Malraney too"
"My father died in Vietnam and that is why I'm here." There were 30 of us this day and we each carried
roses, more than a few.

Three young scouts were there and joined us adults and older vets, too.
We talked as we added the prepared paper tributes to the roses that will honor some we never knew.
But we knew what kind of people they were; they believed in the Red, White and Blue.
Red roses are for K.I.A. and Yellow for M.I.A.
We have even added White for Iraqi Freedom today.
Jan Scruggs, Sons and Daughters rep. and the US Surgeon General all had their say
Then we were off to the Wall to place the roses there on this special clear day.
Tears fall as we read the tributes and touch their names and pray for
Fathers and those who might have been fathers who we should honor today and every day.
Each year for the past ten years, Father's Day has meant to me "Roses at the Wall"

VETERANS DAY

For twenty-four consecutive years since 1982, veterans of the Vietnam War and other past conflicts have participated in the annual Veterans Day observance at the Vietnam Veterans Memorial in Washington, D.C. The Annual Veterans Day observance is hosted and cosponsored by the Vietnam Veterans Memorial Fund and the United States National Park Service. Thousands of veterans and their families come from across the country to attend this annual national ceremony, which includes musical tributes to Vietnam veterans, speeches, wreath laying, and the reading of the more than 58,000 names on the Wall.

Veterans Day 2003 marked the tenth anniversary of the Vietnam Women's Memorial. Veterans, family, and friends honored and remembered the more than 250,000 female military women, nurses, journalists, and Red Cross workers who were the unknown and unsung heroines of the Vietnam War. On Veterans Day, the names of the women who died in Vietnam or since the end of the war were read at the memorial.

In 2005, the fortieth anniversary of the battle of the Ia Drang Valley in November 1965 was commemorated. General Peter Pace, USMC, Chairman of the Joint Chiefs of Staff, delivered the keynote speech.

1959

CHRISTMAS TREE
DECORATION CEREMONY

Each winter holiday season, a few days before Christmas, the Vietnam Veterans Memorial Fund volunteers and staff decorate a Christmas tree at the highest point of the Wall. The tree is decorated with thousands of holiday messages and Christmas cards for veterans and active-duty military personnel. The cards honor the individuals, and their families, who served with the U.S. Armed Forces in Vietnam and other military conflicts.

THE WALL THAT HEALS

On Veterans Day in 1996, the Vietnam Veterans Memorial Fund unveiled a half-scale replica of the Vietnam Veterans Memorial Wall in Washington, D.C. This replica is designed to travel to communities throughout the United States. Since its inception, it has traveled to more than three hundred communities in the United States. In April 1999, the exhibition made its first-ever international journey to Ireland to honor the Irish-born servicemen who were casualties of the Vietnam War as well as all Irish Americans who served in Vietnam.

To further education about the Vietnam Memorial and the Vietnam War, *The Wall That Heals* also features a traveling museum and information center. The museum chronicles the Vietnam War as well as the unique and spiritual healing power of the Vietnam Veterans Memorial. At the information center, people obtain information about friends, family, and relatives who served in the Vietnam War.

ACKNOWLEDGMENTS

Along the way, so many kind individuals helped make this project a reality: family, friends, and to my surprise, more often than not, complete strangers. Those involved with the Vietnam War, whether veterans, friends or family member of veterans, or volunteers, are a special breed. They are some of the most dedicated and loyal people I have ever met.

Jan Scruggs of the VVMF was more than helpful and accommodating in providing information and much of the substance for this project. It could not have been completed, or even started, without his help. Mr. Scruggs and his very generous staff helped locate letters, furnished photographs, offered advice, and spent countless hours on the phone trying to help get this project going. Alan Greilsamer and Lisa Gough were both instrumental in the collection of materials for this book and I can't thank them enough. The VVMF also introduced me to Duery Felton, curator of the Vietnam Veterans Memorial Collection and Pamela Beth West, director of the facility.

On several occasions, Mr. Felton would take the time to offer advice and answer any questions I might have. The entire staff at the National Park Service Museum Resource Center generously offered any assistance necessary. And special thanks to Maya Lin who took the time to consider and support this project.

Special thanks to the unfailing helpful and accommodating literary team for getting this project off the ground. David Stanford offered assistance and encouragement at the proposal stage. Thank you to Jim Levine, and the team at the Levine-Greenberg Literary Agency, who took a chance on an unknown author. Elisabeth Dyssegaard, Janet Evans-Scanlon, and the staff at Smithsonian Books/HarperCollins believed in this project and in the message behind it.

To the volunteers like LTC Anthony V. Fasolo, USA (Ret), I would like to extend my sincere gratitude. He, like my father, not only survived Vietnam but also the September 11 attacks. LTC Fasolo views volunteering as a continuation of his tour in Vietnam, and sees it as his duty to his country and fellow soldiers. To Sharon Denitto, whose efforts to help families and friends of veterans and POWs/MIAs are first class.

To individuals such as Lester Paquin and Joyce Miner, who are dedicated to the memories of fallen heroes, and to all who leave artifacts at the Wall, thank you for keeping the memories alive.

Thank you to the marketing offices, public relations, and community outreach departments of the United States Marines Corps, United States Army, United States Navy, United States Air Force, and United States Coast Guard for their support.

On a more personal level, friends and family provided inexhaustible resources and support. I am forever grateful to them. Brian F. Gredder displayed his usual patience researching and reviewing contracts and answering my questions. To my brother Matthew for his help, support, and being the best little brother a guy could have. To Vietnam veteran Donald Delaney USMC (Ret), and my mother-in-law, Carol Sweeney, who took the time to read letters, offer opinions, and help out in any way they could. And to all family and friends, I thank you.

Without Darren Orr it is very possible this project may never have been finished. I thank him for his words of encouragement and for helping me to see the importance of the book. "D"—thanks for knocking some sense into me.

Sincere gratitude to the United States Marines and the Platoon Corpsmen of Alpha Company 1/4, 1st and 2nd platoons, who were "in country" that February night in '67 and helped my father when he needed it the most. *Semper Fi.*

And of course, to my mother and father. Thank you for being there whenever we needed you. Thank you for being the best parents anyone could ask for. There is nothing I can say or do to properly thank you for all you have done for us now and growing up. In a time where everyone looks to a celebrity or a sports figure as his or her hero, I look to you. You are my heroes. If I can be just half as good as a parent to my son as you were to me, then I will be grateful. You both truly inspire me to be a better person. Thank you.

And to my wife and best friend, Leigh, who offered words of encouragement, advice, and tolerated stretches of neglect so I could finish this project. To my son, Dylan, who has taught me what life is really about and what truly matters. I am so fortunate to have two very special people in my life. I love you both more than words can say.

FOR MORE INFORMATION

Proceeds from the publication of *Letters on the Wall* are being donated to several organizations in an effort to help maintain the collection and support other important programs relating to the Vietnam Veterans Memorial. If you wish to make a contribution, please contact one of the following organizations.

**Vietnam Veterans
Memorial Fund**
1023 15th Street, NW
Second Floor
Washington, DC 20005
Telephone: (202) 393-0090
Fax: (202) 393-0029
www.vvmf.org

**National Park Service
National Capital Region**
U.S. Department of the
Interior
1100 Ohio Drive SW
Room 134
Washington, DC 20242

**The Letters on the Wall
Foundation**
P.O. Box 27
Farmingdale, NY 11735
www.lettersonthewall.com

If you have information regarding an item left at the Vietnam Veterans Memorial, please send a description of the item, the date it was left at the Wall, where it was left, and any other relevant information to:

**Vietnam Veterans
Memorial Collection**
National Park Service
Museum Resource Center
3300 Hubbard Road
Landover, MD 20785